NEW FRONTIERS IN FIBONACCI TRADING

Charting Techniques, Strategies, and Simple Applications

MICHAEL JARDINE

Foreword by
Russell Arthur Lockhart, Ph.D.
Undergroundtrader.com

MARKETPLACE BOOKS
Columbia, Maryland

ISBN 1-59280-061-0

Printed in the United States of America.

CONTENTS

CONTENTS

PART FOUR
BUILDING GOOD TRADING HABITS

PART FIVE
ENTHIOS REALTIME: PUTTING IT ALL TOGETHER

ACKNOWLEDGMENTS

Many thanks to friends and traders who helped, and are still helping me learn how to trade. They include: Brach, Brooke, Buffy, Cambo, Cantro, Chas, Citizen, dave be quick, David, Dawntrader, DPLNeural, Eddie, Fitz, Flea, Garth, Hellcat, Howard, Hunter, Jay, Jimmer, Kimball, Mary, Matt, MSG, Nitro, NQoos, p8, Quartz, RAL, Ramon, rdeux, reifen, Richard, Skylynx, SteveP, Tac, Tradebambu, Trader zone, and Tyab.

Portions of Chapters 2, 3, 4, 6, 17, 18, and 20 appeared previously in *Trend Times* magazine, which is published online by KingCambo.com

Charts in this book are reprinted with permissions from Ensign Software and from Erlangerquote.

Finally, thanks to Jaye Abbate at Traders' Library for the support and patience to produce this book, and to her editorial and production team for somehow making it appear as if I know how to write.

FOREWORD

As a long-time instructor of trading techniques, one of the greatest joys I derive from teaching is being able to witness the transformation of students from confused, even wary participants into confident, successful traders. An even bigger pleasure comes from watching that rare student who becomes absolutely gripped by fascination. Such students, when led by an intense curiosity, often chance upon processes of discovery that lead to a greater understanding of the field and, ultimately, to the making of important contributions to the field. It is gratifying to see these exceptional students transform into the "next generation" teacher.

Such has been my pleasure in watching this development with Michael Jardine. He advanced from avid student of the markets, to the developer of several critical new trading concepts, and now to the "teacher" you will find in the pages of his convincing and powerful new book, *New Frontiers in Fibonacci Trading: Charting Techniques, Strategies & Simple Applications.*

On some level, we are *all* students. Whether it's on the football field, in the office, playing a hand of bridge—or in the trading "pit"—we all were uninitiated novices at some point. We've

all had to work hard to better understand our field, as we've en-
deavored to perfect our skills. I remember the sheer excitement
I felt when I first learned to trade. But I also remember the
frustration and self-loathing I experienced when a trade went
bad. This disappointment fueled my drive to learn from my mis-
steps and find creative solutions to prevent failures from recur-
ring. I began to study everything I could on trading, and I read
up on the methods employed by the most successful traders. I
took courses from trading coaches, watched videos and net-
worked with other traders at industry seminars and online chat
rooms. Eventually—I not only improved my knowledge and
skills—but I began to develop new methods that allowed me to
filter what I had learned and bring it to a brand new level.

Michael Jardine, you'll find, has mirrored this same path on
his road from "green" student of the markets, to professional
trader and author. He has honed and refined his skills over the
years. He humbled himself by seeking the input and experi-
ences of others in his Enthios.com chat room. He then assimi-
lated and learned from all the information he accumulated,
using it to develop new methods and actually strike new "frontiers" in trading. Hence, the title of his new work.

But, as every trader—new or experienced—knows, it's easy
to be overwhelmed by the shear volume of trading methods,
schemes and systems constantly vying for the trader's attention.
In Michael's new book he has performed a radical culling, narrowing down and simplifying all of the "noise" you typically
find in the marketplace. Instead, he focuses strictly on *what
works*. He presents a system that is grounded, logical and
proven. His descriptions of methods are clear and practically
oriented. He outlines in wonderful detail the many charts and
examples he provides. The numbered explanation of trading
events is an extraordinarily powerful device that facilitates not
only learning the methods, but the necessity of strict discipline
so you can *apply* what you've learned in an objective, non-emo-
tional way.

Most importantly, Michael Jardine is a truly passionate teacher, and one can always learn best from a teacher who loves the work. He has written a fine book that I enthusiastically recommend to any trader who has lost his way—as well as those new to trading who are in great need of *finding* a way. And best of all, you will learn here what all successful traders ultimately must learn: "that the master teacher is always the market herself!"

Russell Arthur Lockhart, Ph.D. ("ral" online)
Lead Instructor and Chief Technical Analyst
Undergroundtrader.com

INTRODUCTION

The Greek word *enthios* means "to be inspired by the spirit within." It is the origin of the word *enthusiasm*. There is no better word to describe why we pull objectives seemingly out of the blue and then set about attempting to achieve them: to climb a sacred mountain in a remote corner of Central Asia, or to jump on a train in Singapore just to see how long it takes to reach the Arctic Circle (30 trains and 60 days), or to step unarmed into the most dangerous and colorful bazaar this side of Scheherazade, the electronic marketplace. Online trading is a virtual world of steely-eyed cut-throats, back-stabbers, snake-charmers, master illusionists, secret alliances that shift with the wind, and the unpredictability of pure chaos.

I started enthios.com at the time I started to learn about online trading. It was a place to store all of the information that I was gathering about different charting programs, online brokers, trading methods, technical analysis, links, people, and the entire financial Diaspora. I set up the basic navigational structure as a number of closets into which I could sweep information as it came along. The advantage of having virtual closets is that they are limitless and everything does not come tumbling out when you open the door. However, at some point, one needs to go through the closets and determine what is useful and what is not. This leads to another advantage of having virtual closets;

friends rummaged through them for me, and they then told their friends to do the same. They provided feedback and also asked questions about the material I was storing in there. Those questions helped to teach me how to trade. I learned what other people were looking for, and I learned what their problems were. I learned that in answering their questions, I was getting answers myself. Being a pack rat, I needed a place to store the questions and answers, so I started a discussion group on Yahoo. It quickly grew to over 1,000 active users and is one of the largest groups that allows an open discussion of trading topics.

At about the same time as I started the forum—as the market became more and more difficult to trade, and as it began to sink into the doldrums that were then accelerated by the events of 9/11—I came to the conclusion that simple is best. I did some spring cleaning in the enthios.com closets and came up with what you see here, a concise book for traders. This is by no means all you need to trade; everyone needs to first study a vast array of techniques before deciding to use this method as their primary approach to the market. It is not a beginner's book; nor is it a detailed explanation of technical analysis. In it you will find a systematic approach to trading. And in true systematic fashion, each chapter leads to the next and each section leads to the next.

Let's not overlook the importance of many other methods, however. This system will not appeal to everyone. Many prefer fundamental analysis as their primary market decision-making tool; others prefer to combine aspects of fundamental and technical indicators, using them together. The Fibonacci method and approach is based on the assumption that there is a mathematical sequence in nature that makes events—like stock prices—predictable to some degree. These classic techniques have been endorsed and used by some of the world's top traders and continue to apply to today's ever-changing markets. However, this theory should be recognized as just that. It is only one of many possible points of view.

Part One, **Fibonacci Basics,** begins with what I consider to be the building blocks of price action: market structures and growth and retracement patterns in combination with Fibonacci basics.I then introduce the practical uses of those building blocks and patterns. Part Two, **Practical Fibonacci Applications,** introduces some new and original applications of the Fibonacci sequence that have emerged since the advent of online, real-time trading. I then take a break from Fibonacci and move on to Part Three, **The Chartworks.** This is a selection of helpful analytical tools from the virtual closet of Enthios.com. Once you have all these tools in hand, it is equally important to know what to do with them, and how to put them together into an effective trading system. Part Four, **Building Good Trading Habits,** does just that. Finally, I put it all together in Part Five, **Enthios Realtime.** Here I introduce several new methods that form the core of my Objective Method Trading System, combining Fibonacci, chartworks, and methodical trade analysis.

A WORD ON CHART TYPES

Throughout this book, I use both bar charts and candlestick charts. Bar charts, common on Wall Street and other Western markets, show the high and low as well as the open and close of the time period. Candlestick charts, which originated in Japan, are easier to read because the open and close make up the "body" of the candle, whereas the high and low form the smaller "wick." Candlestick charts have the added advantage of also indicating whether the closing price was higher or lower than the open price, by the color of the candle body. With this information—open, close, high, low and direction—and the exact juxtaposition of those five elements—the Japanese have created a detailed methodology for categorizing and predicting price movement. Candlestick charting has been around for many hundreds

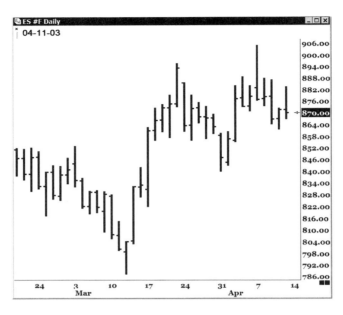

Figure I.1 Comparison of Bar and Candlestick Charts, Same Time Period. *Source:* S&P 500 Emini, Daily, CME, March–April 2003.

of years, far longer than Western markets. One of the best books on candlestick charting is *Japanese Candlestick Charting Techniques* by Steve Nison.

The components of the Japanese candlestick are the fat part which is called the candle *body,* and the thin part which is called the candle *wick* or *shadow.* The body is the range that is bound between the open and closing prices. The wick that extends above the body is that portion of prices that was above the open and close range. It represents failure or testing; that is, prices extended beyond the open price to that high, but then ended up closing back down lower. Likewise, the wick that extends below the body to the low, is that portion of prices that was below the open and close range. In most cases, it is the open and close that are more important; therefore, the body is wider and easier to see visually.

One disadvantage of candlesticks is that because of their bodies, they take up space on a chart. Sometimes it is more useful to use bar charts, particularly in the shorter time frames (less than 30 minutes per candle/bar) where, some argue, the predictive nature of candlesticks becomes less reliable. In this case, it is also possible to color bar charts in different ways, such as rising (close is greater than open) and falling (close is lower than open).

Throughout this text, unless mentioned otherwise, all charts—both candlestick and bar—are black for falling prices (close is lower than open) and white or shaded for rising prices (close is higher than open) (see Figure I.1 on page 4).

ONE QUICK DISCLAIMER

Alas, nothing is completely original. Particularly, nothing that you read in this book or that you will find at enthios.com is completely original; both represent my interpretation of a collection of ideas, methods, discussions, and teachings from other traders whom I have met or read along the way. In this book and at en-thios.com, I have done my best to credit other traders with ideas that I got from them. I am quite sure that I have missed some of the credits, for which I hope they will forgive me. I am equally sure that some traders who read about some of these concepts and methods will say, "Wait a minute, that's *mine*," or "Hey, that sounds familiar" or "That's just called something else." Again, apologies. Try writing an original blues tune that does not use one of the standard four chords! Finally, in some cases, I may have credited another trader or writer for the source of a piece of information or a method. That does not mean that the credited trader is the sole inventor of that method or idea; it only means that I got it from that person. The only thing that is truly original is your own interpretation of the methods that are discussed in this book.

Happy trades to you!

MICHAEL JARDINE

PART ONE

FIBONACCI BASICS

Trading was simple in the old days before the Internet and the advent of online, real-time, intraday trading. Charts did not move; they were completely static because they were made up of daily data only. Investors and speculators analyzed them at their leisure, made their decisions, and then called their brokers who placed the orders the following morning.

Online trading is far more complex; the dynamic nature of multiple time-frame charts, cross-referenced by indices and ticks, all changing second by second and often producing contradictory signals, can paralyze even the most experienced trader into inaction. Throw into that the plethora of technical indicators—moving averages, oscillators, pitchforks, patterns, and the hundreds of variations on these—and the trader is faced with information overload.

On top of that, the equities trader has to worry about searching for "hot stocks" that are about to break out or break down or split or announce this or upgrade that. So in addition to all of the charts changing moment to moment, you have to also contend with screens popping up with lists of stocks that are reaching new highs; or new lows; or strong sector, strong stock; or weak sector, weak stock; and much more.

I have sorted through this array of information and summarized the important elements in a few basics. Everything I use to trade is in this one concise book. I use only a few simple methods and a few simple charts. And it all starts with the Fibonacci basics that are shown in this first section.

I trade the index futures because they are a more pure form of the underlying stocks that they represent, without the machinations of market makers. They are also more liquid. However, the methods that you will learn in this section apply equally to any instrument over any time frame, be it MSFT, the Japanese Yen, or pork belly futures, on a daily time frame or a 1-minute time frame.

1

BUILDING BLOCKS

Everything in nature is made up of building blocks. Just as the universe is made up of atoms, so the market is made up of basic units called *Market Structures*. And just as there are two basic forms of matter within atoms—protons and electrons—so in the market there are two types of structures, **Market Structure Low (MSL)** and **Market Structure High (MSH).** Most price movement in the market can be defined in terms of MSL's and MSH's, and the juxtaposition of the two. Likewise, everything you find in this book is defined in terms of MSL's, MSH's, and the patterns that they form together, 123 Reversals.

In this chapter, we demonstrate how specific price *patterns* develop, and how these can serve as signals for trading decisions. Remember, though, that an isolated pattern indication is only the starting point. A scientific approach to using my method should always include the development of confirming signals. The MSL and MSH are only intended to prompt further investigation and should not be thought of as sure-fire signals compelling immediate action. When a pattern indicator shows up on a chart, you need to then seek out a confirmation pattern to justify a decision to buy or sell.

MARKET STRUCTURE LOW

The reason to follow price patterns is to look for signs that an existing trend is about to change directions. Chartists believe that, in varying degrees, price movements and trends are predictable based on established patterns. Two important concepts should be remembered in all of the following examples: *support* and *resistance* are the keys to understanding how trading ranges and pricing trends work.

A support level is the lowest price that is likely to be seen within a specific *trading range.* As long as a trend continues unchanged, the support level will be observed and prices will not break out below that price level.

A resistance level is the opposite: it is the highest price that is likely to be seen within a specific trading range. As long as a trend continues unchanged, the resistance level will be observed and prices will not break out above that price level.

A trading range is not always a specific price level, but can be a gradually climbing or falling range. In any event, the range can be recognized as a pattern and chartists continually seek signals that a trend is reversing. Many stocks and indices exhibit low volatility and an established trading range will not change over an extended period of time. The value to any form of charting is going to be found in recognizing previously established trends as well as the departures from those trends. Being aware of the concepts of support and resistance, you should expect to see reversing indicators more often in the more volatile issues rather than in the lower volatility ones.

A Market Structure Low (MSL) is the first sign of a potential reversal in prices from a downtrend to an uptrend. It is usually made up of three consecutive candles: A low, a lower low, and then a higher low. The low is measured from the actual low of the candle, not the closing price. Ideally, as shown in Figure 1.1, the low and lower low will both be down bars (where the closing price is lower than the open price), whereas the third bar, the higher low, will be an up bar.

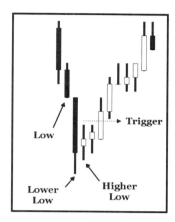

Figure 1.1 MSL.

The MSL is actually *triggered* when prices subsequently move above the high of the third candle, as shown by the dotted line. It is dangerous to enter a long trade simply on the trigger of a MSL. But this book is filled with ample opportunities to use the MSL and MSH as triggers for different trades.

A MSL can also be made up of two bars or candles when they both have the same low. This is known as a **double bottom,** as shown in Figure 1.2. The double bottom is one pattern

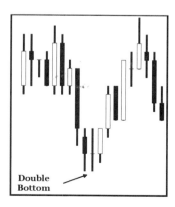

Figure 1.2 Double Bottom MSL.

indicator that most chartists recognize as a strong indicator signaling or predicting a change in price direction. Ideally the first bar of the double bottom will be a down bar, and the second will be an up bar. In this example, the second is a *doji* (open and close were the same), which is neutral.

Not Quite the Same as a Swing Low

Some traders might argue that a MSL is the same as a "swing low." This is like saying that a square is the same as a rectangle. A MSL is more specific in that the third candle acts as a trigger point for considering a long entry or for exiting from a short trade; it is also the defining point of the potential directional change.

MARKET STRUCTURE HIGH

The opposite of a MSL is a Market Structure High (MSH). It is the first sign of a potential reversal in prices from an uptrend to a downtrend. A MSH is usually made up of three consecutive candles: A high, a higher high, and then a lower high. The high is

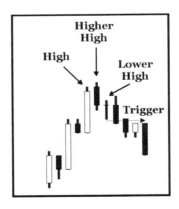

Figure 1.3   MSH.

measured from the actual high of the candle wick or shadow, not the closing price.

Again, the MSH is triggered short when prices move below the low of the third bar in the MSH pattern (Figure 1.3).

Likewise, some traders might argue that a MSH is the same as a "swing high." It is not. Think of a MSH as a "swing high with a trigger."

123 REVERSAL PATTERNS

The next important building block is made up of MSL's and MSH's in combination. Just as a MSL is the first sign of a potential reversal in prices, the combination of an MSL, an MSH, then a *higher MSL,* is a confirmation pattern that a downtrend has reversed into an uptrend. This is illustrated in Figure 1.4.

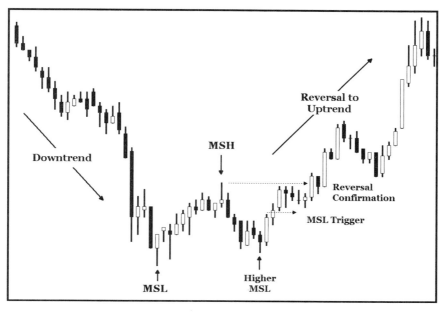

Figure 1.4 Upside 123 Reversal.

The MSL trigger on the higher MSL is one possible point of entry for a 123 reversal trade; however the reversal is not *confirmed* until prices move above the high of the previous MSH. Obviously, hindsight makes this analysis far easier than it is to make the same observations as a trend begins to emerge. As with any method, the Fibonacci system is accurate as long as you are a skilled interpreter. This is why the confirmation pattern is essential in order for you to use this charting method effectively.

2

THE ITALIAN MONK AND HIS PROCREATING RABBITS

In the twelfth century, there was a monk named Leonardo Fibonacci who studied the procreation patterns among rabbits. He observed an elegantly simple numerical sequence that explained the rate of increase in their population.

The sequence starts with zero and one, and then adds the latest two numbers to get the next one. So zero plus one equals one, one plus one equal two, one plus two equal three, two plus three equal five, three plus five equal eight, and so on (Figure 2.1).

This sequence can be used to describe an amazing variety of basic growth patterns of nature, from the distances of the planets from the Sun to the rings of a tree to the proportions of the human body to the branches of the Sneezewort Plant (Figure 2.2).

Just why this simple sequence describes so many different processes of nature has been the subject of debate among philosophers and mathematicians alike for the past seven hundred years. Perhaps even more mysterious is how the same Fibonacci sequence also pops up, with astounding regularity, in the financial markets. Indeed there are many other sequences and formulas that traders use to tell them when to buy and when to sell, but none describe the market so universally, and none translate its chaos into clear meaning so simply and elegantly as the Fibonacci sequence.

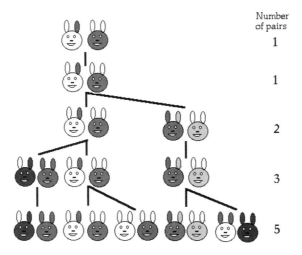

Figure 2.1 Rabbit Procreation Chart.

The Fibonacci sequence is based on the assumption that there is a common thread connecting nature with the markets, and that is the notion of the *seed*. Virtually all of the patterns in nature that are described by the Fibonacci sequence have seeds of one kind or another. Likewise, growth in the financial markets comes from seeds of a sort.

Figure 2.2 Fibonacci Sequence in the Sneezewort Plant.

SO HOW DOES IT ALL RELATE?

To see how Fibonacci's rabbits can tell us when to buy and when to sell 500 shares of Microsoft for a profit, let's look at the first numbers in the Fibonacci series:

1   2   3   5   8   13   21   **34**   **55**   89   144   233   377

There is an intriguing set of interrelationships between these numbers. For instance, any given number is approximately 1.618 times the preceding number and 0.618 times the following number and 0.382 is the inverse of 0.618. (Note that these constants do not apply to the first several numbers in the sequence; however, the further along you move in the sequence, the closer the ratios get to 1.618 and 0.618.)

Just as 1.618 and 0.618 describe the relationship between one numerical value and the next in the Fibonacci sequence, so they also describe the relationship between one surge in prices and the next in the stock market. If a price surges from 5 to 8, then you can multiply the 8 × 1.618, to estimate that the next surge in prices will be to 13. Likewise if the price retraces from 13 to 8, by multiplying 8 × 0.618, you can estimate that the next retracement will be to 5. We have to assume that a similar relationship will be found in price movement, whether the direction is upward or downward. Thus, an original price change to the downside would be expected to move at a rate of 1.618, and a reversal to the upside would advance at the 0.618 rate.

Continuing that logic, just as the ratios between any two successive numbers in the Fibonacci sequence are important, so are the ratios between any *three* successive numbers, and any *four* successive numbers:

$$1.618 = \frac{89}{55}$$

1   2   3   5   8   13   21   **34**   55   **89**   144   233   377
1   2   3   5   8   13   21   **34**   55   89   **144**   233   377

$$\frac{34}{13} = 2.618 \qquad \frac{233}{55} = 4.236$$

Table 2.1 Key Fibonacci Growth and Retracement Ratios

Fibonacci Sequence	Growth (Targets)	Retracement (Pivots)	Inverse (Pivots)
2	1.618	0.618	0.382
3	2.618	0.382	0.618
4	4.236	0.236	0.764
Other	1.382	0.500	0.500

[handwritten margin notes: any two #, any Three #, any 4 # in series]

This gives us additional ratios of secondary importance (0.382 and 2.618), and tertiary importance (0.236, 0.764 and 4.682), as summarized in Table 2.1.

The table also shows two other numbers that are important in the Fibonacci sequence, 0.5 and 1.382. The first—0.5—is an important retracement ratio because it is halfway between 0.382 and 0.618. The midway point is always important in any growth cycle. In the financial markets, when prices drop to the midpoint of a previous trading range, the buyers and sellers will notice this and, collectively if not consciously, pause to decide whether price levels are likely to move back up again, or to continue on down.

PRICES DO NOT MOVE IN A STRAIGHT LINE

Before we apply the ratios in Table 2.1 to the market, let's look at the relationship between growth and retracement because this is important to understanding how prices move in the markets. Luckily for traders, prices do not move in a straight line. The "dips," or retracements, are what provide us with the opportunity not only to enter the trade, but also to estimate when to get out of the same trade.

Generally, when buyers outnumber sellers, the price goes up. This, of course, attracts more buyers—and more willing sellers—until the buying pressure is exhausted. Then prices usually *retrace,* in the direction from which they came. This occurs because the buyers have switched sides to become sellers in order to take profits. These sellers now outnumber the buyers and are chasing the price back down. In a trending market, this tends to have a rubber band effect; each *advance* is met by a *retracement.* After the sellers have taken their profits, if the overall uptrend is still intact, the retracement will then be met by another *advance.*

The combination of an advance, a retracement, and another *higher* advance forms a **wave pattern,** as shown in Figure 2.3. Note how the wave pattern is made up of a MSL, followed by a MSH, followed by a higher MSL. This is the basic building block of any wave: MSL, MSH, higher MSL. For a downward wave, the pattern is simply the reverse: MSH, MSL,

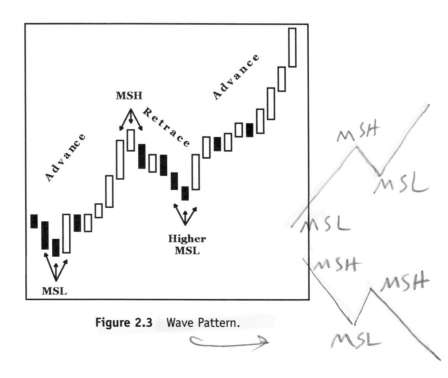

Figure 2.3 Wave Pattern.

and lower MSH. The first wave in a sequence is known as the **seed wave** because it is the seed from which the subsequent waves grow.

The term *seed wave* occurs frequently in physics but was first introduced as a term in financial technical analysis by Russell A. Lockhart, PhD.

The ratios that we derive from the Fibonacci sequence can be used to both gauge the *retracement* of one wave and predict the *advance* of the next. All we need to know is the size of the first seed.

Figure 2.4 shows the same wave pattern as Figure 2.3, but in the slightly more chaotic context of the real world: an actual chart of Microsoft:

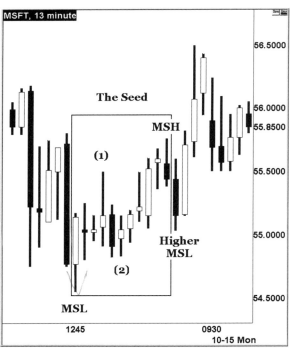

Figure 2.4   Wave Pattern in MSFT. *Source:* MSFT, 13-minute, Nasdaq, 10/15/01.

- Note again the pattern of MSL, MSH, and higher MSL.
- Note also that this wave pattern is the beginning of a reversal from a downtrend to an uptrend (from short to long), so it is a seed wave.

You may also have noticed that reference (1) is a MSH and reference (2) is a higher MSL. Why not use these as the seed? There are many different ways to determine a wave. Strict observers of the Fibonacci sequence contend that there should be between eight and thirteen time periods—both key Fibonacci numbers—between the first MSL and the next higher MSL. This gives the wave a "reasonable" amount of time to develop. Strictly speaking, then, the MSL labeled (2) occurs *before* the eighth candle and so is not counted.

USING FIBONACCI TO FORECAST WAVES

Now that we have identified a seed wave, we can use the Fibonacci growth ratios to estimate how high the next wave(s) will be. This is useful because it tells us when to exit the trade. Note that the ratios do not tell us with any certainty that there *will* be a subsequent wave. They only tell us what to do *if* there is another, higher, wave. Even if there is a subsequent, higher wave, they do *not* tell us with any certainty that the wave will reach the projected Fibonacci target or, if it does, that it will not continue much further beyond. What the Fibonacci sequence does tell us, very clearly and within the law of averages, where the most ideal place is to exit our trade.

Figure 2.5 shows the same 13-minute chart of Microsoft, with the Fibonacci growth *targets* and retracement *pivots* drawn in.

(1) This is the beginning of the wave, as determined by the MSL. Because it is also the low point of the previous trading range, it is the start of a seed wave. At this

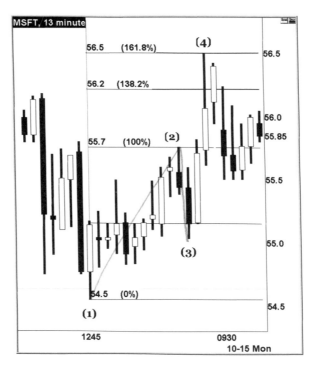

Figure 2.5   Fibonacci Growth Targets. *Source:* MSFT, 13-minute, Nasdaq, 10/15/01.

point, we do not yet have any idea whether a reversal will occur. We only know this in hindsight.

(2) This is the end of the first wave up, as determined by the MSH. Subtract the price at the bottom of the wave from the price at the top of the wave to get the range. In this case, the range is $55.76 - 54.55 = 1.21$. Note how this range is shown in the drawing tool on the chart, with (1) as 0% and (2) as 100%.

(3) This is the higher MSL. It also represents the *retracement* back down from the initial advance to the MSH. Typically, if prices are moving upward with strength, the *retracement* will be to about 50% of the range of the previous wave. This is the previously mentioned point where

buyers and sellers take pause and try to decide what to do next. As you can see in this example, the main candle bodies of the MSH found support at the 50% retracement pivot. After the third candle of this MSL has closed, we have the first *indication* of a trend reversal from short to long. After the MSL triggers long (prices move above the high of the third candle in the MSL), we have *confirmation* of a trend reversal. This is also one possible entry point for a long trade. Once prices subsequently move above the previous MSH, at point (2), we finally have *registration* of the trend reversal. It is important to understand this three-step process: indication, confirmation, and registration.

(4) This is the end of the next advance. Once prices retrace to point (3), and once we see them pivot and move on up, we can then use the Fibonacci targets to estimate where the top of the next wave will be. The calculation is easy. Take the range of the seed wave, which we already know is 1.21 and multiply that by the Fibonacci ratio of 1.618 to get 56.5. That is the target for the growth of the next wave up. As you can see, prices rose exactly to that target before falling back.

$$4 = 3 + 1.618\underbrace{(2-1)}_{1.2}$$

This was an ideal example. On any given day in the market, the trading action is such that you rarely witness a retracement to exactly 50% of the previous wave, followed by a growth to exactly 161.8% of that wave. But you will find that in strongly trending markets, this ideal is the rule more than it is the exception. Shortly, I will take you through some trades that are not quite as ideal.

A WORD ABOUT PIVOTS

Let's take a closer look at that retracement from the MSH down to the higher MSL. Figure 2.6 shows a close-up of the same range as Figure 2.5, but with the key Fibonacci **retracement pivots** drawn in.

It is important to note that when prices fall to the 50% point, there is no guarantee that they will go back up. Indeed, if you think about it, if there *were* a guarantee that prices would go back up, they would not have retraced as far as that point in the first place. That is why they are called pivots. You do not know what will happen at a retracement pivot. What you do know is that at one or more of the Fibonacci pivots (0.764, 0.618, 0.50, 0.382, and 0.236), prices will pause. Like a basketball player, they will *pivot,* then either shoot or run on. This uncertainty is where your analytical skills and experience come in

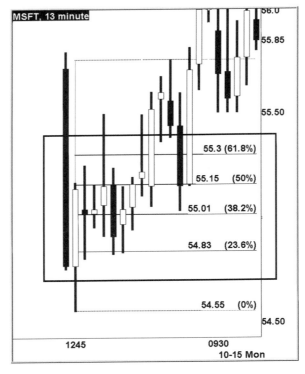

Figure 2.6 Retracement Pivots. *Source:* MSFT, 13-minute, Nasdaq, 10/15/01.

to play. Ultimately, you need to determine based on several factors whether prices will continue or retreat at this pivot.

In Figure 2.6, the main body of the MSL candle found support at the 0.50 pivot (shown in the chart as 50%). The wick/shadow of that candle reached down to the 0.382 pivot. That indicates that when the price dropped to 50% of the range of the seed wave, buyers and sellers started to hesitate. A bear sentiment pushed the price further down but met resistance at the 0.382 pivot before finally giving up when the candle closed at the 0.50 pivot. During the next period, a bull sentiment took over. As soon as that happened, the Fibonacci system calls for the price to go to 56.5 before the next major retracement.

If you had bought 1,000 shares of MSFT at the trigger point of $55.76 (a standard MSH-failure long trigger, described on page 38) and sold at the target of $56.50, you would have earned a profit of $740 (before trading costs).

WHAT COMES NEXT?

Once the seed wave is complete and you have taken your profit, you may have some questions: "What do I do next? Will there be another wave up? What happens if prices reverse back down? How do I tell the difference between a retracement down in an uptrend, and a bearish reversal?"

During the Great Depression, a market speculator by the name of R. N. Elliot came up with a method of quantifying and classifying the seemingly random undulations of mass psychology that we call the financial markets. In a nutshell, a cyclical pattern often occurs in which an upward trend is characterized by a pattern of five waves upward and three waves downward. To clarify, "five waves upward" is actually a five-wave swing pattern made up of three successively higher peaks (MSH's) with two successively higher troughs (MSL's) in-between. When a stock is down trending, the reverse pattern is true, that is, five waves downward followed by three waves upward. An up-trending pattern is shown in Figure 2.7.

In Figure 2.7, that first wave extending from "0" to "1" is called W1. The correction wave down is called W2. Waves 1, 3, and 5 are the main waves in the trend, whereas waves 2 and 4 are the counter-trend, or **correction waves.** The waves a, b, and c are correction waves against the main trend. Wave 1 is the seed for the subsequent waves, upon which the Fibonacci growth ratios are applied to come up with targets for potential waves 3 and 5.

These patterns have forecasting value—when five waves upward have been completed, three waves downward will often follow, and vice versa. By integrating the Fibonacci ratios into the five-wave pattern, price goals can be calculated. I call this pattern *eWaves* in deference to R. N. Elliot.

ANOTHER EXAMPLE

Following up on the wave theory example, we next look at the structure and identify the waves on a chart of the S&P E-mini futures (ES). The next three charts—Figures 2.8, 2.9, and 2.10—all show different ways of looking at the same price action.

Figure 2.8 shows the retracement pivots drawn on the range of the first wave. Prices retrace to 61.8% of the range before

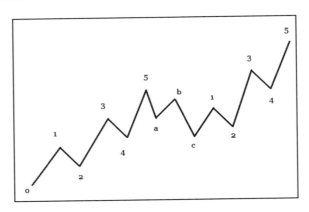

Figure 2.7   eWaves.

continuing on up. This indicates a strong uptrend. Note that there were several attempts to reach the 50% pivot, but that overall the 61.8% pivot held as support.

From Figure 2.8:

(1) Prior downtrend indicates that any reversing movement will be an uptrend, a new seed wave.

(2) MSL forms the potential reversal.

(3) MSH forms the top of the potential seed wave

(4) Prices retrace to the 0.618 pivot, which is the higher MSL. Note that the candle wicks/shadows extend below the 61.8% support lines, but the bodies remain above.

(5) At the point where prices move up above the previous MSH (3), the trend reversal has *registered* and the wave

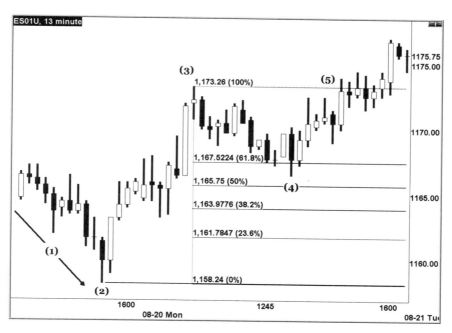

Figure 2.8 Retracement Pivots and the Seed. *Source:* S&P Emini, 13-minute, CME, 8/21/01.

pattern is in place. We can now take the range of the seed wave, 1173.25 – 1158.25, and multiply that times 1.618 to get the growth target of the next wave.

Refer to the wave count in Figure 2.7 and apply those to the pattern in Figure 2.8:

(2) is the "0" point of the first seed wave.

(3) is the top of the first wave, W1.

(4) is the bottom of the second (retracement) wave, W2.

(5) is the confirmation of the third wave, W3.

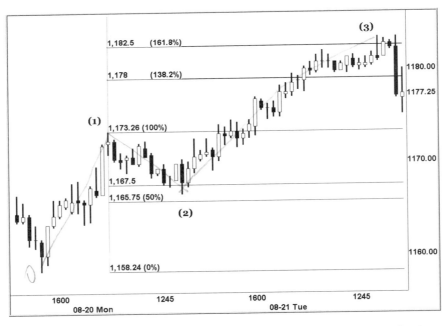

Figure 2.9   Three-Wave Pattern. *Source:* S&P Emini, 13-minute, CME, 8/21/01.

Figure 2.9 shows where W3 actually ended up. It also shows the retracements from W1 and the Fibonacci targets of 1.382 and 1.618. Note how nicely they match up. Waves 1, 2, and 3 are shown as (1), (2), and (3), respectively.

It is important to understand that after a W2 retracement, prices do not always extend beyond the top of W1 to form a W3. In such a case, the wave pattern is not registered. Instead, prices are bound within the previously determined trading range. Even if a W3 does register, there is no guarantee that it will reach the 1.618 target. For example, there may be important price levels just below that 1.618 target that would impede prices from reaching higher. You should always be aware of important price points near a Fibonacci target, and always err on the side of caution when fine-tuning your exit target. Also be aware that statistically, the 138.2% Fibonacci target will get hit more often than the 161.8% target. This is common sense, since it is a closer target. Instead of using fixed targets, it makes sense to use *target zones* for both wave and retracement targets. Typical bands are shown in Table 2.2:

Table 2.2   Fibonacci Target Zones

Wave 3	1.382–1.618
Wave 5	2.236–2.618
Continuation retracement	0.382–0.500
Reversal retracement	0.500–0.618

- A **continuation retracement** is a correction wave that retraces to less than 50% of the previous range, and then continues back up. Typically, though not always, this is representative of a continuation move in the direction of the prior trend.

- A **reversal retracement** is a correction wave that retraces more than 50% of the previous range. Typically, though not always, this is representative of the beginning of a reversal in direction of the prior trend.

Whether the 138.2% target gets hit sufficiently more than the 161.8% target to make up the difference in potential profit, is an important question. It is a constantly changing variable and the serious trader will keep careful notes of all trades in order to keep tabs on which of the Fibonacci targets is a better fit for which equity or instrument, over which time period. Chapter 15 deals with this question in more detail.

THE QUESTION OF THE 8-13 WAVE COUNT

When you try to identify growth waves on your own, you will find that it is not as simple as it may appear; indeed, sometimes it seems as if there are as many different interpretations as there are traders. This is an inherent problem to any charting technique. Your ability to interpret the data is the determining factor in its effectiveness. The value of Fibonacci is that in most cases, the applicable ratios will apply to whatever *your* interpretation is. For example, Figure 2.10 shows that a different interpretation of the same chart can also yield a profitable trade.

Figure 2.10   Five-Wave Pattern. *Source:* S&P Emini, 13-minute, CME, 8/21/01.

THE QUESTION OF THE 8-13 WAVE COUNT

In Figure 2.10, Point (3) is what we previously called W1 in Figure 2.9. But notice that there is a MSH at point (1) in Figure 10, followed by a higher MSL (2). This is the first sign of a 123 reversal. Note also that there are eight candles between the first MSL (0) and that next higher one (2), which qualifies this as a seed wave among those who prefer to use the 8-13 bar count. (Those of you who are mathematically clever will have already figured out that if there are less than 8 bars between the start of W1 and finish of W2 on your 13-minute chart, you can simply increase the number of bars by moving down to a lower time frame such as an 8-minute chart!)

(0) This is the same bottom as in Figure 2.9.

(1) This is the first actual MSH, and so becomes an alternate interpretation of the W1 seed.

(2) A higher MSL forms here, signaling an earlier entry than in the trade in Figure 2.9. This becomes W2. Once prices turn upward, confirming the seed wave structure, we can use the Fibonacci ratios to target the top of W3.

(3) In this case, prices almost reach the 161.8 target but not quite. This illustrates one reason why 1.382 is also an important Fibonacci ratio. If prices move past 138.2 but do not quite reach the 161.8 target, then you can use 138.2 as a stop exit on the way back down. As in the previous example, it is important to look at other price points that may be acting as resistance below the Fibonacci target. Any point within the 1.382 to 1.618 range is a good place to take profits. Thus, the use of the price range between these points can be viewed as a decision range, rather than using either level as absolutes.

(4) In this interpretation, point (4) is the W4 retracement. We will have already made one successful trade before we even recognized the three-wave pattern in the Figure 2.9

interpretation. After the MSH is formed here, we can re-enter the position and can use the next higher Fibonacci ratio of 2.618 to target the high of this W5. Note how this 5-wave pattern fits the eWave diagram shown in Figure 2.7. Figure 2.10 also illustrates one nature of W5 extensions: They tend to be more complex and less dependable than W3. Psychologically this makes sense because you always have more traders jumping on the band wagon (for W3) after the seed wave (W1); W5 is the "third push" up and traders tend be undecided or expecting a possible reversal back down.

(5) W5 is reached at the Fibonacci target of 2.618 × the range of the seed wave.

A NOTE ON FRACTALS AND DIFFERENT TIME FRAMES

Just as Fibonacci growth targets and retracement pivots work in these examples, they also work across all time frames. The two examples just discussed are on a 13-minute chart. If you looked at a 3-minute chart over the same time period, you would see smaller wave patterns embedded within the trading range. Likewise, if you zoomed out to a 30-, 60-, or 135-minute chart, you would see that this three-wave pattern is but one aspect or segment on larger scale wave patterns. Buffy's article on price action, in the appendix, talks more about using different time frames.

SUMMARY AND REVIEW

If you have never considered what the Fibonacci system can indicate, it is worth reviewing the major attributes of that system:

- The Fibonacci sequence is 1, 2, 3, 5, 8, 13, 21, 34, etc.

- Prices do not move in a straight line. They tend to move in waves. The combination of an advance, a retracement, and another higher advancing pattern forms a wave pattern. This is indicated by a MSL, a MSH, and then a higher MSL.

- The first wave in a sequence is known as the seed wave because it is the seed from which the subsequent waves grow.

- Many Fibonacci traders believe that there should be no less than eight and no more than thirteen, candles making up the seed wave (counted from the first MSL to the next, higher, MSL). You can switch time frames so that the seed wave is always between eight and thirteen candles; the time frame that matches this will usually be the best time frame in which to trade that wave pattern.

- The key Fibonacci retracement pivot ratios are 0.236, 0.382, 0.50, 0.618, and 0.764. (These can also be expressed as percentages 23.6%, 38.2%, 50%, 61.8%, and 76.4%.) When prices retrace after establishing a range, they will usually "pivot" at one or more of these points. If prices are going to move back up, ideally they will pivot near the 0.50 retracement level.

- A retracement pivot will act as support level until prices break below it, at which point it will then act as resistance level against prices trying to move back up. Prices are attracted to previous support or resistance just as a moth is attracted to light. As such, they are excellent targets for exiting a trade.

- The key Fibonacci target ratios are 1.382, 1.618, 2.236, 2.618, and 4.236. Typically 1.382–161.8 is used as the *target zone* for W3, and 2.236–261.8 as the target zone for W5.

- The eWave pattern shows that when prices are *trending* upward, they normally move five waves upward and three waves downward. If the uptrend remains intact, it will then resume with another five waves upward, followed by three waves downward, and so on. These are fractal in nature and so one large wave up in a daily time frame will be made up of five smaller waves on a 30- or 13-minute time frame, and so on.

- Confirming a trend reversal is a three-step process: Indication (formation of the first higher MSL), Confirmation (trigger of that MSL), and Registration (break of the prior MSH). This applies to a reversal from short to long but also works in the reverse for a reversal from a long to short.

The entire theory, of course, applies to ideal situations. And the situations illustrated are provided to show how the system works, and not to indicate that these movement patterns occur in every situation.

In the next chapter, I go over the nuts and bolts of executing a trade under these ideal circumstances and then I give you some tips on how to handle the examples that do *not* fit the model.

3

RIDING THE PRICE WAVE

In Chapter 2, I introduced the Fibonacci system and the basics of how waves work. Now let's look at the nuts and bolts of trading: entry, exit, stop loss, and when not to enter.

WHERE'S THAT WAVE?

Trading, like any new idea, is always difficult to master for the novice. The beginner usually learns from expensive mistakes, whereas the more experienced investor *should* know how to mitigate risk. You can study the markets until you think you understand everything, but it's a different matter altogether when you put your money on the line and enter a trade. Just knowing *where* to enter the trade is a challenge in itself. Of course, it becomes obvious after the fact, and this can be frustrating. Using waves, particularly the seed wave, can help you to see trades better. However, it still takes both practice and hands-on experience; there is no substitute.

It is always desirable to enter a wave pattern at the beginning of W1 and ride it all the way to its end at W3, and even on to its possible extension at W5. Unfortunately, you can never know for sure that you are in a wave pattern until both W1 and W2 have completed, and W3 has registered by exceeding the high of W1, as shown in Figure 3.1. Remember, chart analysis is always easy in hindsight, but very difficult as trends are emerging.

Referring to Figure 3.1, let's review some key points from the previous chapter:

- The combination of an advance, a retracement, and another higher advance forms a *wave pattern*. This is indicated by a MSL, a MSH, and then a higher MSL.
- The first wave in a sequence is known as the *seed wave* because it is the seed from which the subsequent waves grow.
- A wave pattern is not confirmed until it reaches the *point of registration,* which is one tick above the high of W1.

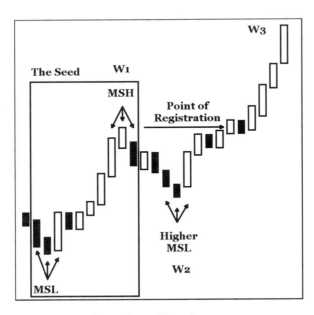

Figure 3.1 Wave Pattern.

ENTERING THE WAVE

The experienced investor might be expected to be able to identify the starting point of the third wave. However, identification of the proper timing is not an easy matter, even for the experienced trader. There are three methods for determining when to time your entry position. Figure 3.2 shows these three methods.

(1) *Pullback trigger:* This is the most subjective, and potentially the most profitable, of all entry methods. If I believe that prices will be heading back up, then this is usually the earliest entry. As prices pull back from the previous MSH, enter one tick above the high of the previous pullback candle. The pullback trigger applies *up to* the *fourth new low* in a price retracement from the

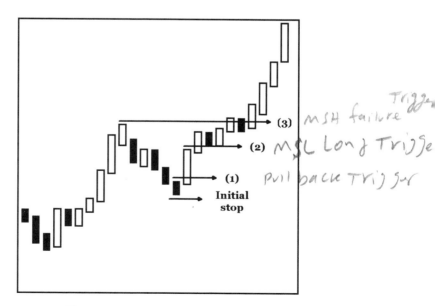

Figure 3.2 Wave Entry Methods.

previous MSH. If prices do resume back up, that fourth
candle would still act as a trigger.

(2) *MSL long trigger:* The MSL is the first objective sign of
a reversal, particularly if the third candle in the MSL is
an up candle, as shown here. This is less risky than the
pullback trigger in the sense that it acts as a confirmation signal, but of course has a correspondingly dimin-
ished reward and higher stop. Enter one tick above the
high of the third candle of the MSL.

(3) *MSH-failure trigger:* The MSH failure can be a very
powerful trigger. Psychologically, it represents the exhaustion point of the previous price run, the point at
which the bulls gave in to the bears. That high price
level automatically becomes a point of strong resistance
on any subsequent price runs, particularly on the first
attempt to break past it. This is also the top of the seed,
the point of registration. Once prices move beyond this
level, they often move quickly and forcefully (remember,
though, that in an opposite pricing trend, that quick
and forceful movement is going to occur to the downside). The MSH-failure trigger is an opportunity, but as
with all opportunities, risks are greater as well.

Remember also that if this second test of the high
fails, that is, the MSH resistance point holds—the result is a **double top,** which in itself is a strong indication of a reversal backdown.

The failure of an expected pattern usually creates another pattern, and often with greater reliability than
the expected one.

WHICH METHOD IS BEST?

The combination of strengths and weaknesses in these approaches have varying risks associated with them, and you need

to determine which one suits your personal risk tolerance. A comparison between entry methods is provided in Table 3.1.

Table 3.1 Entry Methods Compared

Method	Strength	Weakness
Pullback	Highest profit potential, lowest stop loss potential	Highest failure rate
MSL-trigger	Reasonable indication of reversal	Not as profitable as pullback and not as sure as MSH-failure
MSH-failure	Highest success rate	Lowest profit potential and highest stop loss potential

The relative strength can be equated with profit potential, and the corresponding weakness can be equated with risk.

Some questions you may want to ask yourself, as you are trying to determine which method to use, are:

- Where are the key Fibonacci pivots?

- What are your *tier stocks* doing? A tier stock is another stock in the same industry as the stock that you are trading. One stock may start to move first and lead the others.

- What are the indices doing? If you are trading a Nasdaq stock, compare trends among Compx or NDX (Nasdaq futures).

- If you trade in an index, how is one of the leading stocks performing? If you trade S&P futures, for example, you might find that MSFT is a good lead to watch.

- Has there been any consistency in previous price moves? Often the market will develop a short-term pattern of movement that can last for several hours or more. For example, you may notice that all of the **pullback entries** have been successful. Or you may notice that in a jittery market, the pullback entries all fail but that after doing so, prices then continue on up. In that case, a **MSL-trigger** or **MSH-failure entry** might be more appropriate.

SETTING STOPS

Now I have entered the trade. What if it turns against me? This is a good place to talk about the use of stops. A *stop* is a trade exit that is made at a point other than a specific target, and is usually made when the trade turns against you. A *stop loss* tends to be at a loss, but the significance of the name is that it *stops* you from *losing* even more! *Trailing stops* are a good form of trade management to protect gains when your trade is in the profit column. I will introduce both in the following section.

As far as trade execution goes, there are two types of stops: a **mechanical (hard) stop** and a **mental (soft) stop.** A mechanical stop is an order that is placed with your broker to sell your long position if prices move back down to a specific number. Typically a mechanical stop is placed as a *market stop* order; that is, when prices move down to a specific price, the broker then enters a market sell order to exit the position. The advantage of a mechanical stop is that it forces the trader to have thought out the trade in advance and to know exactly at what point he or she will "bail" from the trade. To many, this is comforting because a mechanical stop takes the subjective worry out of trading. Some online brokers offer the ability to mechanically trail stops at a set distance from the most recent high; for example, a trailing stop of 3 points will exit the trade as soon as it retraces 3 points back down from any high.

A mental stop, as the name suggests is one that is placed only in your mind, at least until you decide to exit the trade. It allows you the flexibility to consider other information as the trade progresses. For example, long traders tend to place stops one or two ticks below major support lines (such as a previous MSL). Short traders will also place *sell stop* orders to enter a short trade, at exactly the same price. When prices retrace to the support line, quite often they will then dip below that line, if only momentarily, before resuming back up. This is known as *stop running.* Some traders believe that large institutions or market makers intentionally run stops. Think about it: If you want to take prices up, it makes sense to first push prices back down through a low volume zone by selling, then pick off the large number of traders that are lined up just below the support level like birds on a fence, then force prices back up.

Although there is no doubt that this is a favorite technique of market makers and institutional traders who have the volume to manipulate the market, the fact remains that stop running can occur without any premeditated deviousness; all it takes is one jittery trader or early bird to place a market order at the support point (rather than one tick below it), and prices will drop through, triggering the stop run. By using mental stops, you can avoid stop running but you are also exposed to greater losses if prices continue on down. One way to use a mental stop is to base your stop on the close of the candle or bar. In this way, the wick may extend below your predetermined support level but if the bar then closes back at or above support, you stay in the trade. I will show you examples of mechanical stops, mental stops, and trailing stops in the next few pages.

Here are a few important points to remember (Table 3.2):

1. The use of stops is *highly subjective.*
2. The *tighter* your stop, the more *often* it will get hit.
3. The *looser* your stop, the *greater your loss* when that stop gets hit.
4. The balance between tight and loose stops is an art in itself.

5. Determine, in advance, whether you will use mental stops or mechanical stops. There are advantages and disadvantages to both.

Table 3.2 Stop Methods Compared

	Pros	Cons
Mechanical stop	It can be set and forgotten.	The technique does not allow for *stop running*.
Mental stop	You have the flexibility to step aside from *stop running* and wait for candle to close.	It relies on trader instinct; losses can run excessively.

Figure 3.3 ties together the three-wave entry methods, introduces stops, and shows why it is important to consider key Fibonacci pivots for trade entry and exit.

(1) MSL-trigger entry.

(2) Pullback-trigger entry. Note that in this example, the MSL trigger actually provides an earlier, and safer, entry than the *pullback trigger.*

(3) MSH-failure entry.

(4) The initial stop loss is usually one tick *below* the MSL that generated the MSL buy trigger.

(5) If I used the MSH-trigger entry, my entry point would have been uncomfortably far above the original MSL. Therefore, I might want to use a more recent major MSL, such as the one shown here.

If I had used either the MSL trigger or the pullback to enter the trade, the stop would have been triggered. I could have

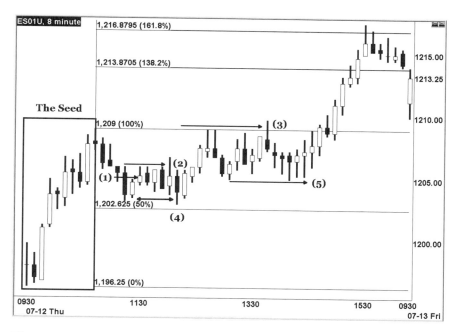

Figure 3.3   Entries, Stops, and Pivots. *Source:* S&P Emini, 8-minute, CME, 7/12/01.

avoided that by being more aware of important price pivots nearby. In this case, the MSL (1) is just a couple of ticks above the 50% retracement of the seed wave. I already know that 50% is a major pivot. When prices drop down that far, they will probably try to test the 50% pivot. So why stop out just a few ticks above the 50% pivot? I may as well wait and see what happens at this point. At point (4), prices did move below the MSL (1) but bounced up just short of the 50% retracement line. If I had waited to see what would have happened once prices hit the 50% line, I would not have stopped out and would still be in the trade.

With clarity of hindsight, at (4) I became a victim of stop running. Instead of placing my stop just below the MSL, I could have used a mechanical stop one tick below the 50% retracement line, or I could have used a mental stop at the point where the bar closed, not at the low.

Look how "they" did the same thing at point (3).

Mental stops work well when price action is made up of traders who are ready to jump out of the trade as soon as prices hit their stop level. Mental stops do *not* work well when prices blow through and don't look back. Unfortunately, it is difficult to tell when to use which; however, by observing the price action of the previous hour or so, you can get a clue as to which method, if any, would work better.

TARGETS AND TRAILING STOPS: EXITING THE TRADE

Figure 3.4 shows the process of going from trade entry, to setting the initial stop, to trailing stops, and then to exit. It illustrates that these are not unrelated actions; once you have committed to the trade, be aware of the relative levels at all times. This process also reinforces the importance of key price pivots and the importance of the MSL and MSH as points of support and resistance.

(1) The initial stop is set at the higher MSL, which is also the 50% retracement pivot. The exit target is $1.618 \times$ the range of the seed wave, but recall from Table 2.2 that it is often better to use the price zone between 1.382 and 1.618 as a *target zone*.

(2) You can use trailing stops at successively higher MSL's first to shorten the stop loss, and then to preserve gains. I prefer to use trailing stops only once prices have reached into the target zone, because up until that point prices tend to whipsaw back and forth between the initial stop and the exit target. Therefore, I would

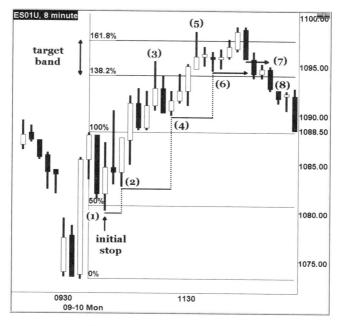

Figure 3.4   Targets and Trailing Stops. *Source:* S&P Emini, 8-minute, CME, 9/10/01.

not use the next MSL shown here. Also, the proximity of the 50% pivot presents a much more significant stop point.

(3) As prices move up, I will begin to look at my Fibonacci exit targets in the 1.382–161.8 band. Here, prices pop up above the 1.382 mark but do not reach 1.618. If this uptrending wave were counter to a greater downtrending wave, then I might chose to exit here at the 1.382 Fibonacci target. If I believe that prices will move up to challenge the 1.618 target, then I would be more likely to hold the trade and look for a support level to form, which it did here at point (4).

(4) Once I have profits in hand, it does not necessarily make sense to give them up altogether. After prices reach into the 1.382–1.618 band, I move my stop loss to my entry point. I move it up once a higher MSL forms, at this point. MSL's always offer a degree of support because they represent the lowest point at which prices were trading at that time.

(5) Sure enough, I am proven correct and prices move back up to hit the 1.618 target. But what if I felt that prices would continue even higher?

(6) In that case, I raise my stop to the 1.382 line, *or* the next MSL, whichever is higher. Here a MSL forms just above the 1.382 line, so I move my stop to this level.

(7) Prices moved back up past 1.618, but this time I was wrong. The earliest opportunity for an exit was one tick below the low of the first **reversal candle.** Not to be confused with the *pullback candle* used as one of the entry methods, a reversal candle is the first "down" candle after a series of "up" candles, that is, a candle that closes below its open.

(8) If I had not used the reversal candle as my exit, I would have exited here based on the raised stop from MSL (6).

Figure 3.5 clarifies the difference between a reversal candle and pullback candles:

(1) *Reversal candle:* First candle in an uptrend that closes lower than it opens.

(2) *Pullback candles:* Successively lower candles from a previous high. Pullback candle trade entry is the first candle where prices exceed the high of any of the previous pullback candles, up to the fourth candle down from the previous high. Entry is indicated by the arrow.

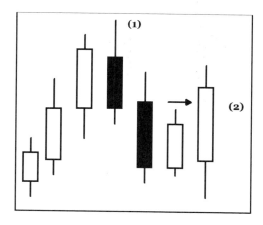

Figure 3.5 Reversal Candle and Pullback Candles.

TRADE MANAGEMENT

You can combine the different entry techniques with trailing stops and with the different exit techniques shown above, by first building up shares on trade entry, then parceling them out during exit. The 8-minute chart of MSFT in Figure 3.6 shows how you might do this. It also illustrates the subjectivity of wave patterns.

In the trade, I assumed that 800 shares was the optimum full load to trade. You will need to determine how many shares to trade based on your own account liquidity and on the relationship between the current price of the stock (or other financial instrument) and its average trading range:

(1) This was the first opportunity for a short entry, the pullback candle. Two clues provided confidence in making this entry. First, on the previous day MSFT completed a W5 extension to the Fibonacci target of

4.236 (shown in Figure 3.7). The *eWave* pattern (see Figure 2.7 for review) indicates that after five waves up, expect a correction of three waves down. So now I was expecting a seed wave to initiate the downward wave pattern. The second clue was the 50% pivot, just one tick below the pullback candle. If prices moved below that, it would be a good sign. And it was. To be safe, I sold short only 200 shares, preferring to wait for further confirmation before going for a full lot.

(2) The MSH-sell trigger provided that confirmation. I added another 300 shares here.

Figure 3.6 Trade Management in the Real World. *Source:* MSFT, 8-minute, Nasdaq, 10/23/01.

(3) MSL failure was the final sell trigger. I added another 300 shares to the short, for a total of 800 shares.

(4) Prices then dropped and hit the 1.618 target. I covered half my shares (400) here and held the rest with a trailing stop. I would cover half of the remaining shares (200) on the next reversal candle and the remaining half on a MSL trigger.

(5) The reversal candle and MSL triggers both occurred here. I covered the remaining 400 shares.

(6) This MSH was a critical point. If I believed the trend would continue down for a W5 extension, I would be looking to short this MSH. If I believed this was an *eWave* a-b-c correction (see Figure 2.7 for review), I would be looking to go long on the next MSL, with (6)-(4) forming the range of the upward seed. I decided to go with the *eWavers* and look long.

(7) My first possible long entry was the pullback trigger, shown here. I bought a small lot of 200 shares, again preferring to wait for further confirmation before buying more.

(8) Here the MSL trigger and MSH-failure trigger were so close that I bought 600 shares at the MSH-failure trigger.

(9) Unfortunately, that was as high as prices reached. This is what I refer to as a *breakout fake-out*. The MSH-failure trigger is normally quite strong but, when it fails, prices will often fall clear to the opposite end of the trading range, as they did here. When prices dropped below the previous MSL (9), which was my stop, I sold all 800 shares.

(10) Once the W3 MSL failed here, the W5 extension registered. I was not expecting a W5 extension, but it happened and so I reacted. I went short 800 shares at one

tick below the W3 MSL, with the W5 target of 2.618 ×
the range of the original seed wave.

(11) Prices dropped right to the target and I covered, making back the money I lost on the previous trade and
preserving the profits from the first trade.

This series demonstrates the importance of interpreting information. It is extremely difficult to identify an ending point
of one trend and the beginning of the next one. In practice, the
Fibonacci patterns would be expected to occur in a dynamic
manner, with trends overlapping and without any specific start-
and-stop points. So as a trader using this method, you will need
to decide on a starting point as your entry, rather than seeking
what would be an artificial beginning to a wave. The effectiveness of your trading skills *always* depends on timing.

USING RETRACEMENT PIVOTS TO
GAUGE A REVERSAL

Once you have identified an ongoing wave, you will want to an-
ticipate its top. In addition to using the Fibonacci ratios to target the top of a wave, you can also use the retracement pivots to
gauge a reversal. This works not just with any one wave, but
also with any series of waves.

Figure 3.6 showed trades on Tuesday, 10/23/01. Now let's
scroll back to the previous day, Monday, to look at the price action leading up to the series of trades we just made. Figure 3.7
shows the two sets of Fibonacci ratios that were first introduced
in Chapter 2: targets and retracements. It also shows the eWave
count for the 5-wave pattern W1 through W5, with the slightly
more chaotic price movement of a real world example.

The first set of lines in Figure 3.7 depicts the Fibonacci
growth targets for Monday. These are calculated based on the

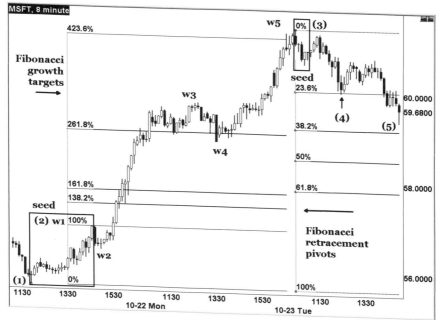

Figure 3.7   Wave Targets and Retracements. *Source:* MSFT, 8-minute, Nasdaq, 10/22–23/01.

range of the seed wave, point (2) less point (1). Note that W1 is *always* the seed. Using a retracement tool found in most good charting programs, you can input the Fibonacci ratios then anchor the range from (1) to (2), and the tool will automatically show the Fibonacci targets of 1.382, 1.618, 2.618, and 4.236 as shown—or any other range multiples that you input.

The second set of lines in Figure 3.7 depicts the Fibonacci retracement pivots. Recall from Chapter 2 that retracement pivots can be drawn on any major range. In this case, I used the same retracement tool with the Fibonacci pivot ratios of 0.236, 0.382, 0.5, and 0.618, and anchored it to encompass the entire range of the price action, from the beginning of the seed wave at (1) up to top of the MSH at (3). This gave me a set of action points to watch during Tuesday's trading. From Chapter 2, you will recall that prices usually do something at each of these retracement pivots. You also know that a continuation retracement from any wave or major range, is 0.382–0.50 of the range. Armed with this information, let's look at Figure 3.7.

Recall that the target zone for W3 is usually 1.382–1.618 × the range of the seed wave, and that the target zone for W5 is usually 2.236–2.618 × the same range. In Figure 3.7, prices shot straight by the 1.618 target and did not stop until they hit resistance at the 2.618 line. At that point, prices hesitated for three candles (24 minutes) before they broke through. When a resistance level breaks, usually it then becomes support. That event is demonstrated clearly in Figure 3.7. Notice how that resistance/support line trends at the Fibonacci target of 2.618. When prices continued up, they peaked at the Fibonacci target of 4.236.

By the time MSFT had surged to 4.236 × the original seed, I knew it was overbought because typically W5 only reaches 2.618. So on Tuesday morning I was expecting at least a 3-wave correction series downward, the pattern that is labeled as "a-b-c" in Figure 2.7. The small size of the downward seed, highlighted in the box in Figure 3.7, at point (3), was not surprising because often after a major breakout there is a period of small range consolidation—*often*, but not always. The 1.618 target for the W3 that would develop from this seed, was only 60.18 (refer back to Figure 3.6 to see the calculation). The retracement pivots in Figure 3.7 show that 60.65 represented only a 0.236 retracement from the previous range. Knowing that the typical continuation retracement is 0.382–0.50 of the previous range, 0.236 seemed weak. Yet that was exactly where W3 hit and bounced, as shown by point (4) in Figure 3.7. The shallowness of this retracement told me that the correction may not be over, that it may take another wave to get MSFT down to the 0.382 zone. In the end, that is exactly what happened at (5).

LAST BUT NOT LEAST

The experienced trader recognizes that there are times to stay out of the market, long or short. Here are three examples of when *not* to trade:

1. Uptrending prices move in an orderly pattern of successively higher MSH's and MSL's. Downtrending prices move in an orderly pattern of successively lower MSH's and MSL's. When these patterns do not occur, as shown in Figure 3.8, it means that there is confusion in the market. It also means that the Fibonacci ratios will be far less reliable.

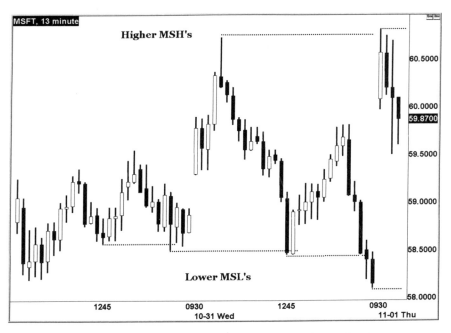

Figure 3.8 Conflicting MSH/MSL's. *Source:* MSFT, 13-minute, Nasdaq, 10/31–11/1/01.

2. When a trend reaches its Fibonacci target and then re-
   verses, as occurred on Wednesday in Figure 3.9, the retracement pivots can be indicated for that trading range.
   One of two things should happen. Either prices will retrace back in to the 0.318–0.618 range (the a-b-c correction in Figure 2.7) then fall back down for a continuation
   of the previous trend, or they will break through the
   0.318–0.618 range for a true reversal of the trend.
   Usually 0.50 is the critical point. In Figure 3.9, neither of
   these occurs. Prices hit resistance at the 0.382 pivot, and
   remained trapped in the range between the previous low
   and 0.236. When this happens, sit back and do something
   else until prices break out of the range one way or the
   other and re-establish the trend.

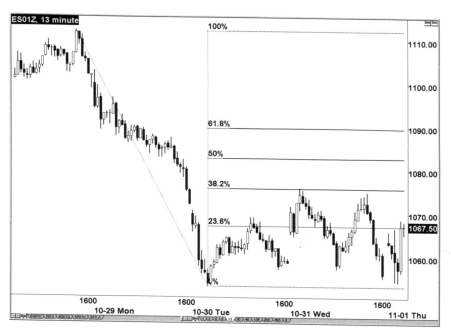

Figure 3.9 Stuck in a Fibonacci Range. *Source:* S&P Emini, 13-minute, CME,
10/29–11/01/01.

3. "Congestion," "consolidation," "narrow trading range": Whatever you call it, you don't want to be trading when there is no clear trend and prices are just drifting sideways. Figure 3.10 shows two ways to recognize price congestion. The first is when you see alternating candle directions/colors, as shown in the congestion box on the left. By comparison, look at the uniform color of the candles in the breakout on Thursday. Another way to recognize price congestion is to use a middle-length moving average, such as the (Fibonacci) 8-period exponential moving average (EMA) shown here. When the 8-EMA bisects the candles and has little or no slope, trading is in congestion. By comparison, look at how the candles all close above the 8-EMA in the breakout on Thursday.

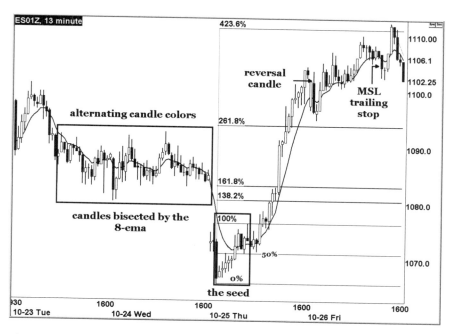

Figure 3.10   Recognizing Congestion. *Source:* S&P Emini, 13-minute, CME, 10/23–10/26/01.

Figure 3.10 also shows two examples of using the reversal candle and trailing stop techniques to extend the trade beyond the 1.382–1.618 target zone.

SUMMARY AND REVIEW

- The combination of an advance, a retracement, and another higher advance forms a wave pattern. This is indicated by a MSL, a MSH, and then a higher MSL.

- The first wave in a sequence is known as the seed wave because it is the seed from which the subsequent waves grow.

- A wave pattern is not confirmed until it reaches the point of registration, which is one tick above the high of W1.

- The three methods of entering an up-trending wave are pullback candle, MSL trigger, and MSH failure. (For a downtrending wave, the latter two become a MSH trigger and MSL failure, respectively.)

- Determine, in advance, whether you will use mental or mechanical stops, and be aware of the advantages and disadvantages of each.

- In trading waves, trailing stops can help protect profits once the 1.382–1.618 target zone has been reached, and as a means of staying in the trade should it break out beyond 1.618.

- Two other exit methods, once the profit target has been exceeded, are reversal candle and MSH-reversal trigger (MSL in the case of a short trade).

- After W3 has completed, sometimes it is difficult to tell whether to look for a long (W5 extension) or a short (new wave series down). Use the *eWave* count 12345-abc-12345 as one means to guide you.

- Also use retracement pivots from the previous wave series, to guide you.

- Do not trade when the pattern of successively higher MSH's and MSL's breaks down (successively lower MSH's and MSL's, in the case of short trades).

- Do not trade when prices are stuck in a low Fibonacci range. 0.382–0.618 are the action areas.

- Do not trade during price congestion. There are many ways to tell. One is by alternating candle colors. Another is when candles are bisected by the 8-EMA.

- The failure of an expected pattern usually creates another pattern, and often with greater reliability than the expected one.

4

INCREASING THE ODDS

In the previous chapters, you have learned how to use the Fibonacci system to gauge retracements between the inflection points of a MSH and MSL. You have also learned how to use Fibonacci to predict W3 and W5 expansions from the seed (W1). The most important Fibonacci ratios are 0.236, 0.382, 0.5, 0.682, 0.764, 1.382, 1.618, 2.618, and 4.236. A retracement of 0.382–0.50 is ideal, and the target zone of 1.382–1.618 is often the best target for a W3, while 2.236–2.618 is usually the target zone for a W5. If you use these ratios consistently, you can trade profitably. You can increase the odds favorably by combining methods. The premise is logical: Use multiple methods to come up with multiple targets. Then see where these targets coincide, to create a *combined target zone.* I touched upon this at the end of Chapter 3 and will expand upon it here.

Figure 4.1 shows how to combine the retracement pivots from a previous range, with the *seed wave targets* of the next, to fine-tune the exit target for W3. The price is most likely to pivot at the 0.382, 0.50, and 0.618 retracements from a prior trading range. The pivots shown along vertical line (d) are calculated from the prior major trading range (a) – (b). After the seed is created, I then draw the Fibonacci expansion targets off that original seed. The downward targets from the seed wave (b) – (c) are shown along line (e). The combined target zone is where the

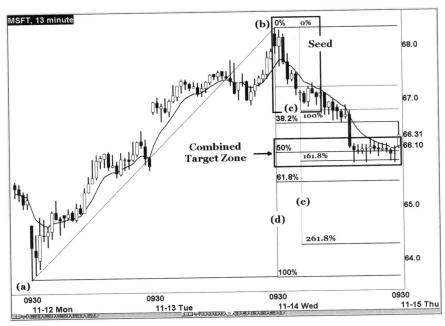

Figure 4.1 Combining Methods. *Source:* MSFT, 13-minute, Nasdaq, 11/12–11/15/01.

pivots and targets from these two sets of lines coincide, in this example, between the 50% retracement pivot and the 161.8% wave target.

The mathematics of the sequence—1, 2, 3, 5, 8, and so forth—explain the growth rate in general terms. But the market is dynamic; it is composed of not just one set of waves moving in a given direction, but of sets within sets. Any up wave series could be contained within a larger down wave series, which in turn could be contained within an even larger up wave series. As a result, it makes sense to incorporate all the information from those other, greater wave impulses, to whatever extent possible.

Short of producing a complicated algorithm that can automatically take all these into consideration and spit out the ideal end target, this method of combining pivots and targets works well. Two more methods of measuring recent wave impulses will further strengthen the probability of the positive outcomes using combined target zones.

SEED RETRACEMENTS

So far, expansion targets have been drawn from the first seed, W1. But why not measure the strength of the retracement from that first wave, in effect the **seed retracement?** The retracement from the seed is always W2. Figure 4.2 shows the Fibonacci targets drawn upward, using the distance from the top of W1 (b) to the bottom of W2 (c), as the basis. This is the calculation:

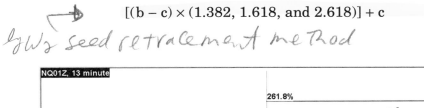

$$[(b - c) \times (1.382, 1.618, \text{and } 2.618)] + c$$

by W2 seed retracement method

Figure 4.2 W2 Expansion Targets. *Source:* Nasdaq Emini, 13-minute, CME, 10/03/01.

Figure 4.3 shows the same chart, but adding the W1 seed targets that you are familiar with from Chapters 2 and 3. To review, the targets are calculated as:

[handwritten: by W1 seed Target methods]

$$[(b - a) \times (1.382, 1.618, 2.618)] + a \quad or$$

[handwritten: $(b-a) \times (0.382, 0.618, 1.618) + b$]

The first set of Fibonacci targets are calculated up from the seed wave (a) – (b). The second set of Fibonacci targets are calculated from the retracement wave (b) – (c), which I call the *seed retracement*.

The zone where the two combined target methods coincide is the combined target zone.

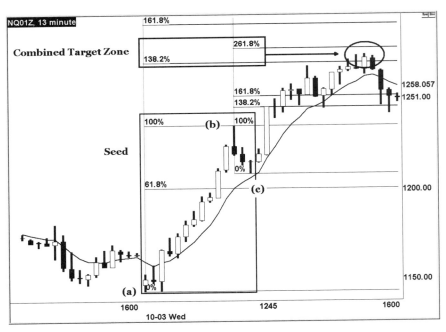

Figure 4.3 W1 and W2 Combined Targets. *Source:* Nasdaq Emini, 13-minute, CME, 10/03/01.

MEASURED MOVES

Measured moves are measurements of the size of a wave, as applied to the size of the next wave in the same direction. Imagine using a ruler to measure the size of one wave, then shifting that ruler over to the beginning of the next wave and cloning that onto the second wave. So if the size of W1, from trough to peak, is 100, then the size of W3 (the next wave in the same direction) would also be 100, as measured from its trough to its peak.

Figure 4.4 shows an actual, though idealized, example of a measured move. The amplitude of W1 is 1516 − 1463 = 53 points. Add 53 to the start of the next wave, 1489 + 53 = 1542. In this

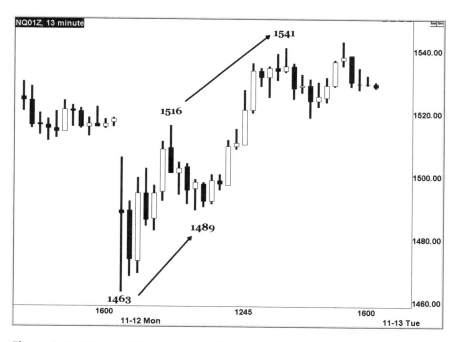

Figure 4.4   Measured Move. *Source:* Nasdaq Emini, 13-minute, CME, 11/12–11/13/01.

case, we missed by one point. The measured size of W3 was 98% that of W1.

The measured size of W3 is not usually the same as W1, though 1.0 is a good starting point for a multiplier. W3 might be smaller, or it might be larger, than W1. So we can use the Fibonacci ratios and multipliers of 0.618, 0.764, 1.0, 1.382, and 1.682 to measure the size of W3 against that of W1, then compare that to any of the three other methods—W1 seed targets, W2 seed retracements, or previous range retracements—to come up with a combined target zone. Table 4.1 at the end of this chapter compares the four different targeting methods.

Figures 4.3 and 4.5 show combinations of two methods. You can experiment to see which combination of Fibonacci targets

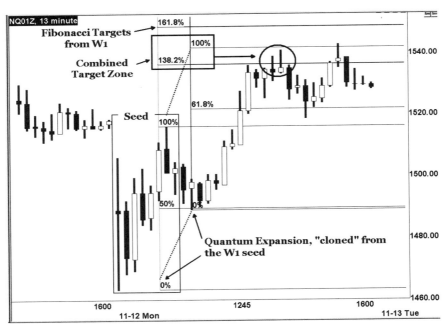

Figure 4.5 W1 (seed) Target and Measured Move as Combined Targets. *Source:* Nasdaq Emini, 13-minute, CME, 11/12–11/13/01.

and ratios work best for you, and when to use which ratios. For example, when W2 is very small or only one or two candles in length, perhaps the W2 seed retracement method will not yield a good combination. Likewise, if prices are not retracing from a previous major trading range, then it would not make much sense to look at prior range retracements for one of your combinations.

MULTIPLE MEASURED MOVES

Just as I used one measured move from W1 to help determine the target zone for W3, I can use the two consecutive measured moves of W1 and W3 to help determine the target of W5. Figure 4.6 continues from Figure 4.5. It shows the measured moves from

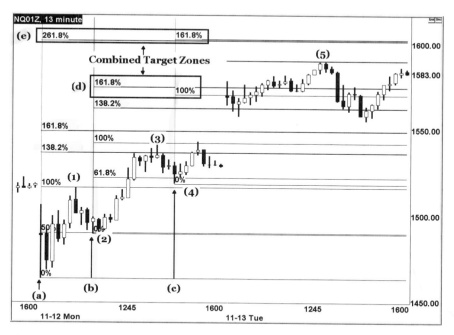

Figure 4.6 Multiple Measured Moves with W1 Targets for Combined Targets Zones. *Source:* Nasdaq Emini, 13-minute, CME, 11/12–11/13/01.

W1 and W3, and well as the original W1 target—three methods altogether—to pinpoint a combined target zone for W5.

The five waves in this *eWave* pattern are labeled (1), (2), (3), (4), and (5), respectively. The first set of lines from vertical line (a) shows the targets from the W1 seed. As always, 1.382–1.618 is the W3 *target zone* and 2.236–2.618 is the W5 target zone.

The second set of lines from vertical line (b) represents the W3 measured move taken from W1. The third set of lines (c) represents the W5 measured move taken from W3.

From these three sets of lines, there are two combined target zones highlighted in boxes (d) and (e). Zone (d) is made up 161.8% of the measured move from W1, and 100% of the measured move from W3. As you can see, on Tuesday prices gapped up into zone (d) then moved slightly higher, proving that even the Fibonacci growth patterns are not an exact science in the chaos of the market.

THE LAST WORD

You may ask why combined target zone (e) in Figure 4.6 was not reached. It appears to be the stronger of the two zones, because the 261.8% target from the W1 seed, and the 161.8% target from the W1 measured move, overlap exactly; they are a perfect match. If Fibonacci were an exact science, wouldn't prices have reached that point? Figure 4.7 illustrates the last word.

SUMMARY AND REVIEW

There are four types of Fibonacci retracements and targets that can be used to create expansions targets for waves. These are prior range retracements, W1 (seed) expansions, W2 expansions, and measured moves. These can be combined to create target zones to increase the probability of targeting trade exits. The four types are shown in Table 4.1 and refer to Figure 4.8.

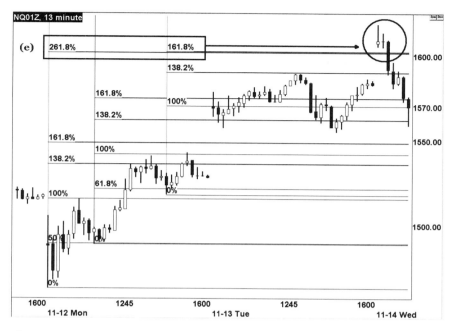

Figure 4.7 Another Look at the Combined Target Zone. *Source:* Nasdaq Emini, 13-minute, CME, 11/12–11/13/01.

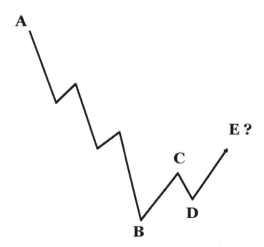

Figure 4.8 Creating Combined Target Zones for Potential Wave DE.

Table 4.1   Summary of Methods to Target Potential Wave DE

Name	Description	Formula
Prior range retracements	Using retracements from prior major range AB	$[(A - B) \times (0.286, 0.382, 0.618, 0.764)] + B$
W1 expansion targets	Using growth targets projected from the seed wave BC (W1)	$[(C - B) \times (1.382, 1.618, 2.618, 4.236)] + B$
W2 expansion targets	Using growth targets projected from the retracement wave CD (W2)	$[(C - D) \times (1.382, 1.618, 2.618, 4.236)] + D$
Measured move targets	Taking the measured size of the seed wave BC (W1) and applying that to potential wave DE (W3)	$[(C - B) \times (1.0)] + D$

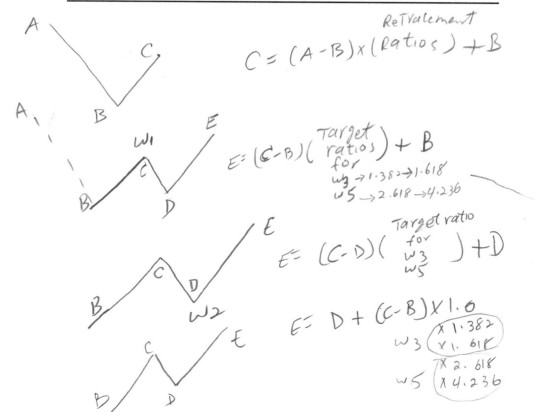

Retracement

$$C = (A - B) \times (Ratios) + B$$

$$E = (C - B)\left(\begin{array}{c}\text{Target} \\ \text{ratios} \\ \text{for}\end{array}\right) + B$$
$$w3 \to 1.382 \to 1.618$$
$$w5 \to 2.618 \to 4.236$$

$$E = (C - D)\left(\begin{array}{c}\text{Target ratio} \\ \text{for} \\ w3 \\ w5\end{array}\right) + D$$

$$E = D + (C - B) \times 1.0$$
$$w3 \left(\begin{array}{c}\times 1.382 \\ \times 1.618\end{array}\right)$$
$$w5 \left(\begin{array}{c}\times 2.618 \\ \times 4.236\end{array}\right)$$

PART TWO

PRACTICAL FIBONACCI APPLICATIONS

NEW AND ORIGINAL APPLICATIONS OF FIBONACCI FOR DAY TRADERS

Like most technical and market analysis tools, Fibonacci was originally applied to static daily charts. However, it can be applied to the intraday chart as well. Over the past several years, both I and a number of trading colleagues have come up with some useful applications that are the direct result of sitting in front of dynamically changing charts on a computer screen. Some of these applications can be "back translated" to the static daily chart; others, such as Citizen's Trading Range, can only be used on an intraday chart. Together, they represent some new uses for old methods, in an everchanging market.

$$E = (C-B)\left(\begin{matrix} 0.382, 0.618 \\ 1.618, 3.236 \end{matrix}\right) + C$$

5

9/11: MONITORING THE WAVE COUNT

The market is dynamic. If we liken it to a pond, the major events of each day are made up of several large stones thrown into that pond. They will send out waves, and some will create a large wake. The most significant points are found where those waves and wakes cross.

At the same time, many smaller stones are constantly being thrown into the same pond. These may be news events, a broker filling a large institutional order, or investor reaction to events in a particular market segment. Each of these stones creates waves of their own initial magnitude, which go out into the pond in increasing undulations until another wave from the other side crashes up against it.

The pond does not start each day with a smooth or undisturbed surface. It has many larger things pushing and pulling and tugging on it. This particular pond is actually a crater lake and sits atop a smoldering volcano. Heat from underneath constantly causes the lake to boil over. Rock slides from above constantly rumble and shake. And earthquakes turn the lake into a dancing caldron.

Each wave, therefore, is affected by, and in many cases, created in part by other waves. Five waves on a one-minute chart become one wave in a three-minute chart, which is one of five waves in a 13-minute chart, which in turn is one wave in a 30-minute chart. You can continue this exploration on to a 120-minute chart and then to a daily, weekly, and monthly chart, and so forth. The opportunity comes in the way we *use* this information in trading.

For example, the 8- or 13-minute chart is a good place to start for trading intraday signals. As I illustrated in Chapters 3 and 4, you do not need to look at any other chart or assemble any other road maps. Just to keep an eye on the bigger picture, though, I also monitor the longer time frames. That way I see where we are—how close we are to a wave target and how close we are to one of the major trading range retracements. I keep a chart specifically for this purpose, which I call my wave count chart. I usually keep it as a 60-minute chart, alternating between that, 30-, and 135-minute charts (405 minutes is the length of the trading day for the futures indices, and 135 minutes divides that day into exactly three periods). I then keep count of the three types of waves on these charts—major, normal, and minor. I track them using three different font sizes, so that I can see the relationships between them all. The most important targets—the ones that line up together—I mark on my charts.

Let's go through this to see how it works. I'll use charts from September 17, 2001, the first day of trading after the longest market shutdown since World War I, and show how we could have pinpointed the low point.

Referring back to Chapter 2, I pull out my Fibonacci ruler and draw the targets on the chart in Figure 5.1. As you can see, W3 overshot 161.8. This happens! On the other hand, W2 retraced back exactly to the 50% line. The waves are marked on the chart as my major W1, W2, and W3.

Let's take the same price action and look for the smaller waves in between by switching to a 60-minute chart, which is shown on

Figure 5.1 Contraction Wave Pattern. *Source:* S&P Emini, 240-minute, CME, August–September 2001.

Figure 5.2. I've erased the major wave target lines, but kept the wave-count markings. You see that the major W1 on the 240-minute chart—which falls between August 24 and August 30—is actually made up of a five-wave contraction series on the 60-minute chart. The first Fibonacci target drawing shows that W3 hit 161.8 exactly but overshot W5.

Notice how major W2, by definition a correction wave, is made up of a three-wave growth series, which exactly hit the 161.8 target. This is exactly the same as the a-b-c shown in Figure 2.7. I only expect three waves on this retracement, because it is in the correction wave of a major contraction wave series.

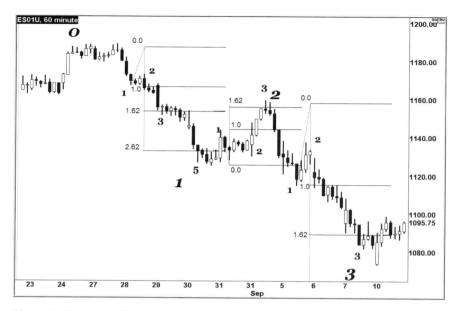

Figure 5.2   Major Three-Wave Pattern with Normal Waves in Between. *Source:* S&P Emini, 60-minute, CME, August–September 2001.

Major W3 is made up of a three-wave contraction series. Prices slightly overshot 161.8, but look at the other bull's eyes it did hit. As of 4:15 P.M. September 10, 2001, we were looking for a major W4 correction, then W5 down. Why? Because we were in a bear market and so the chances of a W5 extension were much greater when prices move in the direction of the trend, which was down. That W4 correction might very well have turned around and become a major W1 in an uptrend, but until we get a 123 reversal on the major 240-minute scale, we are still expecting the W4 correction up, then W5 expansion further back down.

So what will that major W4 be made up of? Just like the major W2, it should be made up of a three-wave growth series.

Figure 5.3 includes the last 12 candles of September 10, as well as the post- and pre-markets to 7:30 A.M. EDT September 11. During the overnight Globex session, prices moved steadily upward. By early morning, it looked as if the 161.8 target of W3, 1200, would be reached shortly after the market's open on September 11. This would have completed the major W4 correction wave and paved the way for the expected major W5 down, in search of the bear-market bottom.

Figure 5.4 shows the price action starting at 8:30. At 8:52, the market began to drop as news of the first airplane hit. The second plane hit at 9:05, causing a 30-point drop before prices rebounded 10 points. The NYSE never opened that day and pre-market trading halted at 9:30.

Figure 5.3 Premarket Trading Activity on 9/11. *Source:* S&P Emini, 60-minute "all sessions", CME, 9/10–9/11/01.

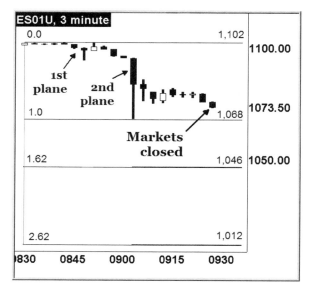

Figure 5.4   Premarket Activity on 9/11. *Source:* S&P Emini, 3-minute, CME, 9/11/01.

In the days after the tragedy, traders sought answers to questions like, "Where will the market open?" and "Where will it bottom?" The Fibonacci series gave us a good idea.

Figure 5.5 shows two W5 calculations. The first is based on the major contraction wave series that we followed in Figures 5.1 and 5.2. The second is from the three-minute chart in Figure 5.4, based on that first 25-point move before the market was closed down. When the market re-opened on September 17, notice how prices found support right between the two W5 targets. Note also how the 161.8 target from the Figure 5.4 also acted as the resistance level for the next two days.

Why did prices bounce at that zone? It is probably that buyers were looking for a point at which to start buying, to prop up both the indexes and the stocks themselves, or simply to buy in

Figure 5.5 Fibonacci and the Effect of 9/11. *Source:* S&P Emini, 240-minute, CME, August–September 2001.

at a favorable price level. It is also possible that this Fibonacci "eclipse" became a self-fulfilling prophecy, since so many traders use it. Growth and contraction waves do not predict nor do they dictate. They simply give us a means of saying *if* prices reach a certain level, *then* something will likely happen. They tell us how to react.

Keeping track of the wave count on a macro and micro basis can help tell you where you stand in the larger, overall market.

6

FIBONACCI AND THE REGRESSION CHANNEL

Take any scattering of points—for example, look up at the night sky full of stars. Now draw a box around them and call it a chart. If you start on the left side of that chart and travel across to the right, and if you moved in a straight line, but in a manner so that your line came closest to each and every star, that would be a regression line. There is a mathematical formula for calculating that line. All you need to know is where each and every star is located.

But perhaps you don't know where they are all located. You can still take those points that are visible and run them through the same mathematical formula. This will produce a line that represents your best estimate for the most efficient path across the universe, even for the part that you cannot see.

The same applies to prices on a chart. By entering the closing prices of a series of bars or candles into the equation, you will produce a trend line that best describes the direction and slope of those candles. This trend line can be used to forecast not only prices into the future, but also the expected deviation from those prices, based on prior price movement.

WAVE CHANNELS

Because price movement tends to oscillate in a series of undulations or waves, it is best to calculate from the trough of one wave to the trough of the next, or from one peak to the next—one full cycle. It is also best to begin the calculation from the point of a price reversal, as shown in Figure 6.1. By now you know that this first wave of a reversal is the seed wave, and that the retracement wave back up is the seed retracement.

There is a formula for calculating the regression line, but most charting software (Table 6.1) will calculate it for you. Most

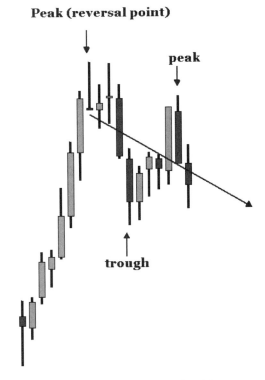

Figure 6.1   The Regression Line.

Table 6.1 Charting
Programs (Incomplete List)

Ensign Windows

Erlangerquote

Esignal

Trade Station

Qcharts

Investor RT

Advanced Get

Sierra Charts

Cyber Trader

MBT

will also draw a confidence channel on either side of the regression line. The most common channel is made up of 2-standard deviations, which statistically includes 95.4% of all prices that were included in the sample series—in this case, that range is found in the first wave from which I measured.

Figure 6.2 shows the same regression as in Figure 6.1, based on the first two peaks of the wave—the first MSH and the next, lower, MSH. It also shows the regression channel of 2-standard deviations. As long as prices remain within the down-trend channel, the trend remains intact. I call this type of regression channel a *Wave Channel*.

There are several ways to use the Wave Channel. You can trade within the channel—essentially, following it down (or up, as the case may be). You can trade the extremes, taking long signals at the bottom and short signals at the top. Or you can trade a breakout of the channel in the opposite direction.

I prefer to trade within the channel—using it in combination with an exit target method such as the Fibonacci multipliers, as shown in Figure 6.3. This allows you to exit the trade toward the bottom. You can, of course, exit the trade once prices move below the bottom of the channel, because at that point

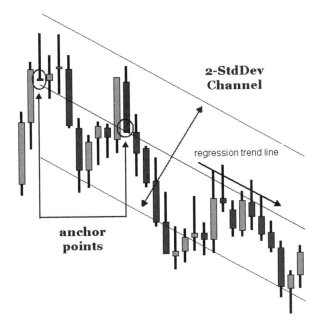

Figure 6.2 Wave Channel.

they have exceeded the 2-standard deviations 95.4% rule and are likely to retrace.

Figure 6.3 illustrates the details of a Wave Channel trade:

(a) The regression channel drawing tool is anchored from the starting point of the reversal, at the MSH.

(b) The trough of the first wave is here. This is W1, the seed wave.

(c) The regression channel drawing tool is then dragged across to this next lower MSH, encompassing the full amplitude of W1 (a – b) and the seed retracement W2 (b – c). The Wave Channel then extends out to the right, predicting prices to the right of point (c) within the 2-standard deviation confidence band.

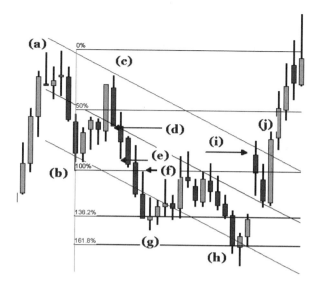

Figure 6.3 Wave Channel Trades.

(d) There are three ways to enter this trade. The first is at this point, when prices drop below the low of the previous candle. This is the **pullback entry** (see Figure 3.2 for review).

(e) The second way to enter is after the MSH has set in place. The trigger is one tick below the low of the third candle of the MSH. This is the *MSH-trigger* entry.

(f) The third way to enter is when MSL (b) fails and prices move below that point. This is the *MSL-failure* entry. In Fibonacci seed wave analysis, this is the *point of registration* of W3.

(g) This is the first possible exit point, where a candle closed below the lower band of the Wave Channel, and where the Fibonacci *target zone* of 1.38–1.62 was reached.

(h) Here is another possible exit, where the ideal Fibonacci target of 161.8% was reached and, again, a candle closed below the lower band of the Wave Channel. However you would have had to sit through a fairly large retracement back up. This underscores the importance of having a clear stop methodology in place. One such method is the reversal candle; another might be one tick above the high of the first candle that touches or exceeds the middle (regression) line.

(i) If you decided to stay in the trade and ride it beyond the target points (g) and (h), your "worst case" stop is the previous MSH. In that case, the stop would have been triggered here.

(j) When prices move up and out of the upper band of the Wave Channel, the downtrend has been broken. You should now be out of the trade. You would then look to draw another regression channel, this time on the trough-peak-trough (MSL-MSH-MSL) of the reversal wave, for the long trade.

REGRESSION BANDS

Another type of regression channel uses Regression Bands to form a dynamically changing channel. This is not anchored to a specific wave; rather, it is dynamically updated based upon the prices over a fixed number of time periods, counting back from the present period. You tell the charting program how many bars you want to count, and it produces the regression channel for you. Because it dynamically updates, the channel will appear as a series of fluid bands, resembling Bollinger Bands, following the price movement up and down.

Figure 6.4 shows a 360-tick chart with 100-bar Regression Bands. (Tick charts are made up of ticks, rather than fixed amounts of time. For more information on tick charts, see the beginning of Chapter 17 and Figure 17.1.) The lines form the

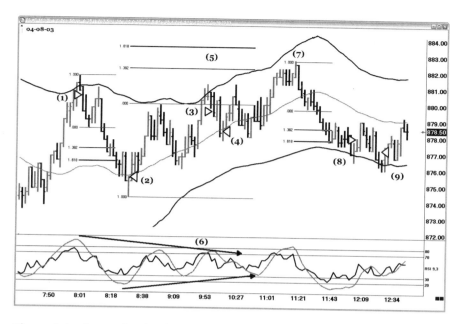

Figure 6.4 Regression Bands with Fibonacci. *Source:* S&P Emini, 360-tick, CME, 4/8/03.

2-standard deviation channel, which means that the likelihood of prices falling within the band is at 95.4%. When prices reach the 2-standard deviation band, there is a very high likelihood that they will retrace back toward the mean. With this knowledge, and with the added confirmation of a stochastic, RSI, or both, you can develop a fairly consistent array of trading methods. One basic trading method is described next:

- *Basic trade:* When prices descend to the lower 2-STD channel, go long. Exit the trade when prices reach the centerline. A safe long entry is one tick above the first *up bar*. An up bar is the same as a reversal candle; when looking for a long trade it is the first candle/bar in a series that closes higher than its open.

- *Basic filters:* Only take 2-STD touches when the sto-chastic is < 20 and looking to cross up or when the RSI is < 30 and looking to cross up. In this example the Sto-chastic is set to 14-5-2 and RSI is 9-3. You may want to adjust these based on your charting program and on the instruments that you are trading. Only trade when there is at least a two point profit potential (in the case of the S&P Emini).

- *Stop:* There are many different ways to stop out of this trade; one is to stop one tick below the first reversal can-dle below your original entry, or below the regression bands, whichever comes first.

Refer to Figure 6.4 and observe how we use our knowledge of Fibonacci to trade:

(1) Prices touch the upper regression band, suggesting a re-versal back toward the main regression line in the mid-dle. Entry is one tick below the low of the first reversal bar, as shown here. As this presumed reversal would also be the beginning of a downward seed wave, we can draw the Fibonacci targets in. Note how they coincide with the regression line. This gives us added confidence. The basic method described above calls to exit at the re-gression line; however, we may chose to exit the trade within the Fibonacci W3 target zone of 138.2–161.8. Either way, it would be a profitable trade. Note also how both the stochastic and the RSI are in agreement.

(2) Trade exited at the regression line.

(3) Our next trade opportunity came when prices touched the upper Regression Band for the second time, as shown here.

(4) The short trade exited here with barely one point gain. There are three reasons why we should *not* have taken

this trade. *First,* the potential profit was less than two points.

(5) *Second,* as shown here, we drew a Fibonacci target based on the first reversal wave beginning at point (2). Because the target zone has not yet been reached, we do not have confidence that upward movement has exhausted itself, despite prices touching the upper regression band.

(6) *Third,* there is a **divergence** between price action and the underlying indicators; both the stochastic and RSI lines are showing a tightening of their oscillation peaks and troughs. The peaks of the oscillations are getting shorter, which is a bearish sign because it shows that although prices are reaching higher highs, they are doing so with less and less conviction. This is a good sign for our short; however, the oscillation troughs are getting higher and higher, just as the waves are reaching higher and higher lows; this suggests that the uptrend is still intact—which is in agreement with what the Fibonacci target is telling us, that the up trend is not quite over.

(7) Sure enough, after this trade, prices made one more push back up, right into the target zone indicated in (5). We did not take the short trade based on regression bands because in this example prices did not touch the upper band. However, we could have taken the trade based on three other pieces of information in this chart: First, the uptrend had probably ended by hitting the previous target zone; second, because of the oscillation peak *divergence* shown in (6); and third, because both the RSI and Stochastic are in agreement. Note how prices then reached the Fibonacci target zone shown at this point (7).

(8) Now that the previous target zone has been reached, we are looking for a reversal long back toward the middle regression line. Entry is shown here.

(9) Not all trades are successful, as shown here. Stop was after the first *reversal bar* below trade entry.

These are just two methods for using Fibonacci to trade regression channels and bands. The creative trader can come up with many methods that suit their trading style, from tick scalping to position swing trading. Because of its simplicity and statistical significance, the regression line is one of my favorite tools.

7

40-EMA AND WAVES

I have found the 40-period exponential moving average (EMA) to be another simple, yet powerful tool. You can use it on its own or as I prefer, you can use it in combination with other methods, such as Fibonacci-based waves. EMA is calculated for you in most charting programs.

Here is how I use it with waves. When you see a wave pattern developing, look for a cross of the price over the 40-period exponential moving average (40-EMA), which can be a good trigger. These are the criteria I look for when going long:

- Before considering entry, wait until you see a candle open and close above the 40-EMA.
- The candle must be an up (bullish) candle.
- Study the chart to make sure that prices have not been consolidating around the 40-EMA line recently but have been breaking above it and below it on pretty good runs.

Note the high of that first candle that opens and closes above the 40-EMA. When prices break above that high, go long.

Figure 7.1 illustrates how to trade this:

(1) When prices break above the high of this candle, enter the trade. Note that this is the top of a potential minor seed wave.

(2) This candle closed entirely above the 40-EMA line. Following the rules of a MSH-failure trigger entry, I would have entered the trade during this candle, before it closed. Using the 40-EMA cross method, I might have waited until this candle closed above the 40-EMA, to ensure that prices had broken out of sideways congestion. Bear in mind, however, that an MSH-failure is usually a strong trigger. So an aggressive entry would have been to take the MSH-failure entry and use the 40-EMA as a stop. The target zone is shown at 138.2%–161.8%.

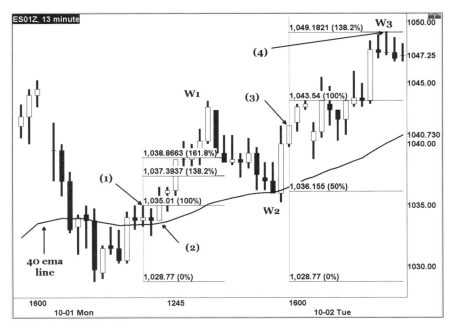

Figure 7.1　40-EMA and Waves. *Source:* S&P Emini, 13-minute, CME, 10/1/01.

(3) This candle closed above the 40-EMA and represents a safe trigger entry for a new long position. At this point, prices have moved into a major wave pattern, as shown by the W1, W2, and W3 indicators. Accordingly, I calculate the Fibonacci targets anew.

(4) Safe exit is the lower end of the target zone, as shown here. A trailing stop could be entered at this point, with the expectation that the upper end of the zone, 161.8%, would be reached. In this case, it was not and I would have stopped at the low of this candle, still with a reasonable profit.

8

FIBONACCI TARGET PIVOTS: SUPPORT AND RESISTANCE

Prices are fickle. They shift allegiances at the drop of a hat. There is a good reason for this. Price movement is simply a direct reflection of the collective psychology of the people who are trading. Price itself does not have a conscious mind and cannot create or shift an allegiance; however, movement does represent the "collective consciousness" of traders in the market.

The concepts of support and resistance are essential elements in price movement analysis and are indispensable to chart reading. People have memories. Mass-trading psychology dictates that if a price looks like it is not going to hold, traders will dump their long holdings. On the other hand, if prices return to earlier support and don't drop below, investors reason that they may as well cover their shorts at that point.

This is why, before the market opens, it is important to mark your charts with the visible support and resistance lines from previous days. If prices move toward those lines during the day, those lines will almost certainly act as important pivot points. You will also want to pay attention as these price lines develop within the trading day; you should mark those as well. Then you will want to use these lines when targeting your trade *entries,* *exits,* and *stops,* regardless of the method you are employing.

For example, let's say you are trading a 123 long reversal and your 1.618 Fibonacci target is 1022. In marking your chart, you notice that 1020 was strong resistance yesterday. Where do you set your exit target? 1020 would be the logical choice because of the importance of that resistance level.

An interesting aspect about support and resistance is that once resistance is broken, that old resistance line becomes support, and once support is broken, that old support line becomes resistance. Figure 8.1 illustrates this.

Notice how resistance (b) becomes support (c) but then, when that support is broken, price allegiances immediately seek out the next place to run to (d), which was the previous support (a). When support is broken at (c), that line immediately

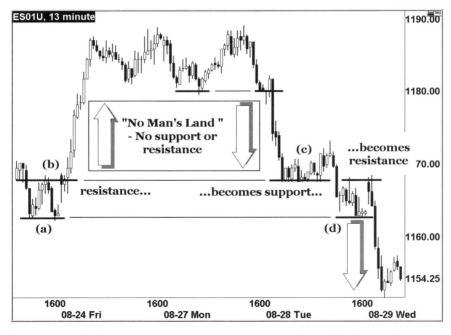

Figure 8.1 Resistance Becomes Support. *Source:* S&P Emini, 13-minute, CME, 8/24–9/29/01.

becomes resistance. It's almost as if traders are thinking, "Since that price didn't hold, I'm not going back there again."

Notice something else. When there are no previous support or resistance lines, a kind of "no man's land" is created, as shown in the areas marked by the three large arrows. When prices broke out above resistance for the first time (b), there was no recent overhead resistance, so they simply rose until buying pressure eased. Support was then created, as shown by the two solid lines, but any trader knew what would probably happen if support were broken and prices re-entered no man's land: Prices would fall, rather precipitously, and straight to the next support level, line (b)–(c). When that broke, prices then dropped to the next rung on the support ladder, line (a)–(d). And when that broke, we knew there would be another free fall through the next "no man's land."

Now look at the price action that occurred at the break-downs of points (c) and (d). Let's zoom in to take a closer look (Figure 8.2).

Each time before prices broke down through support, they first drifted up to touch the resistance line. This is the consolidation range *breakout fake-out*. Some traders call this a "flag" or a "ledge."

The more you look at charts, the more you will see that the breakout fake-out is extremely common, but why does it happen so often? The reason is that traders are sitting at the resistance lines, waiting for long triggers.

As we discussed in Chapter 3, any large institution or market maker that is planning on going short will notice this and would be foolish not to take prices up to sell to all those long day traders before pulling the support plug and bringing prices down to the next level.

This is why I look for 123 reversals and don't play a long breakout the moment it occurs. If I miss a moon shot, it doesn't matter because they are rare. More often than not, I miss the breakout fake-out instead.

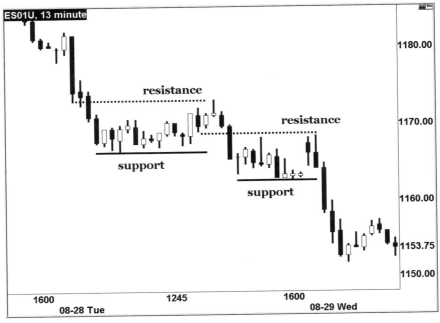

Figure 8.2 Support/Resistance (S/R) on Ledges. *Source:* S&P Emini, 13-minute, CME, 8/28/01.

THE INVISIBLE ENEMY

In addition to these visible lines of support and resistance, there are many invisible lines—that is, lines that are invisible now but that will soon become very visible once prices move across them.

In the next several chapters, I talk about many of those lines, including Fibonacci trading ranges, Citizen's Trading Range, and Gann Angles.

One set of invisible lines are the Fibonacci-based target pivots, which I call "T's" to distinguish them from wave and retracement targets which are drawn based on the distance between two points. I learned about these from Russell A. Lockhart, PhD., one of my trading mentors.

The T's are based on *one reference point* only. You can choose any one point that seems significant to you, such as a major MSH or MSL, but the most commonly used reference point is the previous day's *closing price*.

Start with the basic Fibonacci divisor, 0.382. To bring that number into scale, shift the decimal place over one place (0.0382) for equities and over two places (0.00382) for the larger-scale indices. This becomes the first target (T1). You simply multiply this times the previous day's closing price, then add it to that price to get T1, or subtract it from that price to get –T1. For example, on September 9, 2001, the S&P 500 futures settled at 1039. T1 is 1039 × 0.00382 = 1043. –T1 becomes 1035.

$$T_1 = 1039 + 1039 \times 0.00382 = 1043$$
$$-T_1 = 1039 - 1039 \times 0.00382 = 1035$$

Table 8.1 Target Pivots for Equities and Indices

	Factor	Equity Value	Factor	Index Value
T8	**.662**	**166.20**	**.0666**	**1066.2**
T7	.562	156.20	.0562	1056.2
T6	.462	146.20	.0462	1046.2
T5	**.362**	**136.20**	**.0362**	**1036.2**
T4	.262	126.20	.0262	1026.2
T3	**.162**	**116.20**	**.0162**	**1016.2**
T2	**.062**	**106.20**	**.0062**	**1006.2**
T1	**.038**	103.80	**.0038**	**1003.8**
Closing Price	0	100.00	0	1000.0
–T1	**–.038**	**96.20**	**–.0038**	**996.2**
–T2	**–.062**	**93.80**	**–.0062**	**993.8**
–T3	**–.162**	**83.80**	**–.0162**	**983.8**
–T4	–.262	73.80	–.0262	973.8
–T5	**–.362**	**63.80**	**–.0362**	**963.8**
–T6	–.462	53.80	–.0462	953.8
–T7	–.562	43.80	–.0562	943.8
–T8	**–.662**	**33.80**	**–.0662**	**933.8**

T2, logically, is calculated using 0.0618 for equities and 0.00618 for indices. From that point on, we simply increase the previous T by one increment. So T3 is 0.1618 for equities, T4 is 0.2618, T5 is 0.3618, and so on.

Recall that the Fibonacci sequence is 1, 2, 3, 5, 13, and so forth. I apply this sequence to the targets, which means the only ones I'm really interested in are T1, T2, T3, T5, T8, and T13. In any event, ±T3 is only exceeded on average once every few days and it is quite rare to exceed ±T5.

Table 8.1 shows the T's, using a stock price of 100 and an index price of 1000, for comparative purposes.

Remember, we are only interested in the T's that are bold, that is, those that are part of the Fibonacci sequence, and we usually only deal with T1, T2, and T3 on a daily basis.

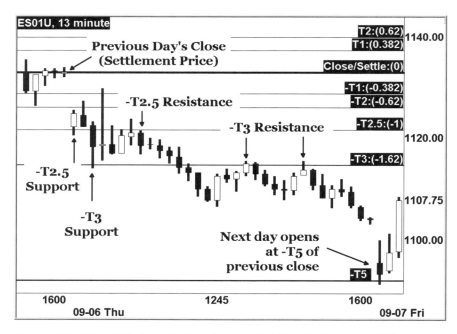

Figure 8.3   Target Pivots in Action. *Source:* S&P Emini, 13-minute, CME, 9/6/01.

My colleague Citizen, whom you shall meet in the next chapter, has added her own "T" to the mix, with a value of 0.01 for equities and 0.001 for the indexes. Since this value falls between T2 and T3, she calls it, fittingly, "T2.5." That price level is often very significant, at least for the S&P futures.

In Figure 8.3, I have plotted the T's on an intraday chart of the S&P500 E-mini futures for Thursday September 6, based on the closing price of Wednesday September 5. Notice the prices gapped down to open at –T2.5, hit resistance at –T2, and immediately went for the next support level, –T3.

This pattern of support becoming resistance, and of the price diving down to find the next support line once a previous line is broken, is a common occurrence in the financial markets. In fact, it is a constant that you can depend on, no matter what method you use to identify support and resistance.

T_1 0.00382

T_2 0.00618

T_3 0.01618

T_4 0.2618

T_5 0.3618

9

CITIZEN'S TRADING RANGE

Citizen's Trading Range (CTR) was developed by one of my trading colleagues, who is known online as "Citizen." It is a simple and obvious tool that is effective and easy to use.

CTR is easy to figure. On a one-minute chart, wait for the first Market Structure High (MSH) and the first Market Structure Low (MSL) to form (Figure 9.1). It does not matter in which order they occur. These signals usually occur within 10 minutes after open and are the first waves of the day—both up and down—the ripples in an otherwise clear pond, caused by the first rock thrown. From these mini market structures, calculate the upside and downside Fibonacci growth targets of 161.8 and 261.8. These four lines give you the positive and negative (*CTR Up* and *CTR Down*) ranges for the day. The result is a very useful channel for gauging the relative strength or weakness of price action during the day. The CTR Up and CTR Down also tend to act as support and resistance lines.

Since the first move is down, we draw the CTR Down lines by calculating $(b - a) \times 1.382$ and 1.618, just as we learned in Chapters 1 and 2. After the next move up, we can then draw the CTR Up lines by calculating $(c - b) \times 1.382$ and 1.618. The resulting four sets of lines represent the upper and lower

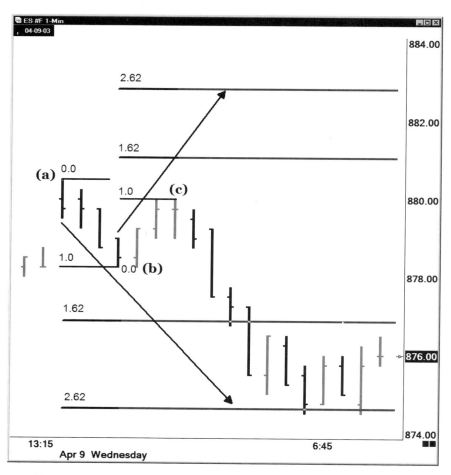

Figure 9.1   CTR Ranges. *Source:* S&P Emini, 1-minute, CME, 4/9/03.

bounds of CTR. They are the first stone thrown into the market pond.

Now let's look at the importance of CTR as the same day unfolds (Figure 9.2). The CTR lines clearly acted as strong support and resistance throughout the entire morning. CTR Down acted as initial resistance after the first move down, then as

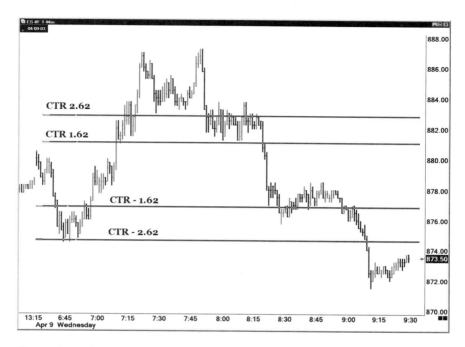

Figure 9.2 CTR as Support and Resistance. *Source:* S&P Emini, 1-minute, CME, 4/9/03.

support on the move back up; CTR Up acted as strong support until 8:15 Pacific Time. When support finally broke, prices moved directly to CTR Down as support. This is not to say that prices will always jump between the CTR lines; only that lacking any other clear Pivots in-between, these will often act as important points and, as such, should be taken into consideration in your trades.

CTR is the first entry that I make on my charts after the market opens. Together with the other important price points, trading ranges, and pivots, it begins to form my road map for that day's trading.

LAST LOOK

A 3-minute chart of the entire trading day shows how the CTR
is useful not just for the morning, but often for the entire day;
Figure 9.3 shows how the late afternoon rally stalled at exactly
CTR –2.62.

Figure 9.3   CTR as Hidden Support/Resistance (S/R). *Source:* S&P Emini,
3-minute, CME, 4/9/03.

PART THREE

CHARTWORKS— VALUABLES FROM ENTHIOS.COM

In one of the virtual closets of enthios.com, I have stored a number of trading methods and shortcuts that do not fit anywhere else in the structure of this book but which remain important or original enough to include. I have adapted some of these materials to my own sensibility—a habit that I encourage all traders to develop.

10

THE PRICE HISTOGRAM

The **Price Histogram** is one of my favorite indicators, because it presents a totally different way of looking at price action than we are normally accustomed to seeing.

The Price Histogram is a graph that shows the relative amount of time spent at each price point during the day. It usually forms a bell curve, with the widest point of the curve representing the price or prices where traders spent the "most amount of time" during the day. This is known as the **Point of Control (POC).** The POC is significant because it represents the price at which traders were most comfortable trading during the day.

The logic behind the Price Histogram is that the majority of a day's transactional volume takes place in a common range of prices, with less trading on the price extremes; and that with this in mind, the important and most revealing information is to be derived from observing those groupings. This is the same premise used in statistical methodology, in which the exceptions, or spikes, are removed from a population of results. By removing those spikes, the remaining information is a more accurate average or representation. Under the Price Histogram, we simply apply the same rule to price ranges, and discount those prices outside of the 70% trading range for the day. This 70% range is known as the **Value Area (VA),** the upper boundary is the **Upper Value Area (UVA),** and the lower boundary is the **Lower Value Area (LVA).**

A typical Price Histogram chart is shown in Figure 10.1, with the POC and VAs indicated. The Price Histogram indicator shown here is available in Ensign Windows. Similar indicators are also available with other programs under different names.

To give you an idea of how the information is gathered, you can create a Price Histogram manually in an Excel spreadsheet by dividing the rows into equal price segments and the columns into equal time segments, say 13 per day (representing 30-minute blocks). Then put a "1" into each cell where the price occurred in the given time segment. To see the bell curve effect, and to ascertain the POC, add a sum column. Figure 10.2 shows the result.

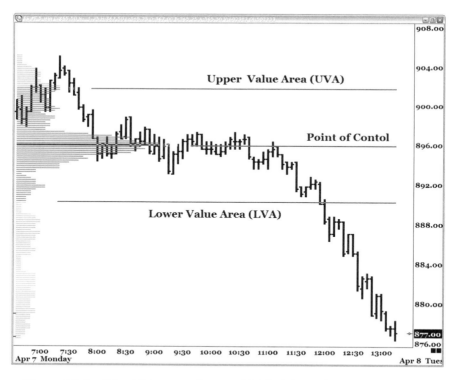

Figure 10.1   Price Histogram. *Source:* S&P Emini, 5-minute, CME, 4/7/03.

A	B	C	D	E	F	G	H	I	J	K	L	M	AA	Prices	Subtotal
9:30-10:00	10:00-10:30	10:30-11:00	11:00-11:30	11:30-12:00	12:00-12:30	12:30-13:00	13:00-13:30	13:30-14:00	14:00-14:30	14:30-15:00	15:00-15:30	15:30-16:00	16:00-16:15	Prices	Subtotal
														1126.5	1
														1126	1
														1125.5	1
														1125	2
														1124.5	2
														1124	4
														1123.5	4
														1123	5
														1122.5	8
														1122	8
														1121.5	10
														1121	11
														1120.5	9
														1120	9
														1119.5	10
														1119	9
														1118.5	8
														1118	7
														1117.5	7
														1117	6
														1116.5	3
														1116	3
														1115.5	3
														1115	3
														1114.5	2
														1114	2
														1113.5	2
														1113	1
														1112.5	1
														1112	1
														1111.5	1
														1111	1

Figure 10.2 Price Histogram in Excel Spreadsheet.

109

TRADING WITH THE PREVIOUS DAY'S PRICE HISTOGRAM

There are many different trading methods that can be derived from the Price Histogram. Some are based on the static position of the previous day's completed histogram; others are based on the dynamically changing histogram during the current day. Some examples of the former follow.

"Down Below" Trade: Downtrend and Open Is below Previous Day's LVA

Sell when prices retrace back up to the previous day's LVA, and again at the POC (if reached) (Figure 10.3). Stop (on the S&P Emini) is 1.5 points above the previous day's UVA. Cover at an obvious Fibonacci target, or the current day's POC, or at the end of the day:

(1) Trade went short here at the previous day's LVA, as indicated by the solid horizontal line.

(2) Trade entered another short here at the previous day's POC.

(3) Stop is 1.5 points above previous day's UVA.

(4) Trade exited at end of day. Note also that as the end of the day is approached, if prices are gravitating toward the current day's POC, that is always a strong price target and therefore a good exit opportunity.

"Down Within" Trade: Down Trend and Open within Previous Day's Value Area

Sell when prices retrace back up to the previous day's UVA (Figure 10.4). Stop is 1.5 points above the Day Before Yesterday's

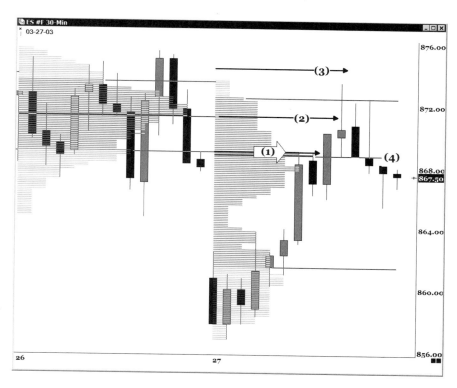

Figure 10.3   "Down Below" Trade. *Source:* S&P Emini, 30-minute, CME, 3/26–27/03.

Point of Control (DBY's POC). Cover at previous day's LVA or other obvious support point:

(1) Trade entered short at previous day's UVA, as shown.

(2) Stop is the day before yesterday's POC, as shown.

(3) Trade covered at previous day's LVA.

(4) If the LVA target had failed, an obvious target would have been 50% retracement of the current day's range, as shown at this point (4). The range is 50% of the distance between the current day's high and low.

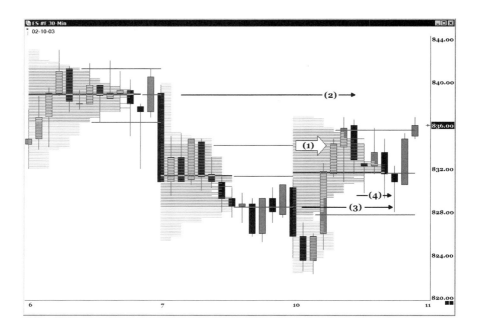

Figure 10.4   "Down Within" Trade. *Source:* S&P Emini, 30-minute, CME, 2/06–2/10/03.

Figure 10.5 refers to the next two trade types.

"Up Above" Trade: Up Trend and Today's Open Is *above* the Previous Day's UVA

Enter long at the previous day's UVA and again at the previous day's POC; stop loss 1.5 points below the previous day's LVA:

(1) First long entered at previous day's UVA.

(2) Second long entered at previous day's POC.

(3) Stop placed 1.5 points below previous day's LVA.

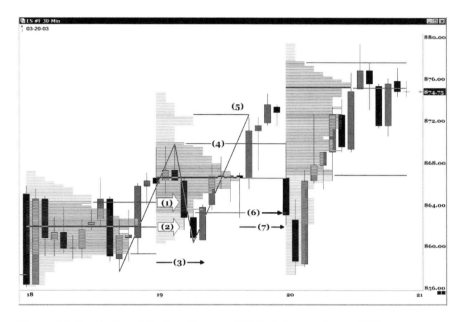

Figure 10.5   Up Trend Trades. *Source:* S&P Emini, 30-minute, CME, 3/18–3/20/03.

(4) Exit at current day's UVA (note this dynamically changes), or at a Fibonacci wave target, or at end of day (EOD).

(5) One such Fibonacci target was the measured move shown here (refer back to Chapter 4, Figure 4.4).

"Up Within" Trade: Up Trend and Today's Open Is *within* the Previous Day's Value Area

Enter long at previous day's LVA; stop loss 1.5 points below DBY's POC.

(6) Entered long at previous day's LVA.

(7) Stopped at DBY's POC. Note however that the traded ended up profitable. One way to re-enter a stopped trade

is to use intraday techniques, discussed in the next section, to enter a long at the current day's LVA.

USING THE PRICE HISTOGRAM FOR INTRADAY TRADING

The Price Histogram can also be used for intraday trading, as it develops "real time" (as opposed to using the previous day's profile). The next several illustrations show one way to trade the Price Histogram intraday.

Usually after the first hour of trading the initial trading range has been set; the "lines" have been drawn in the sand. And the Price Histogram has begun to take shape. Figure 10.6 shows the VA which encompasses the range where prices spent 70% of

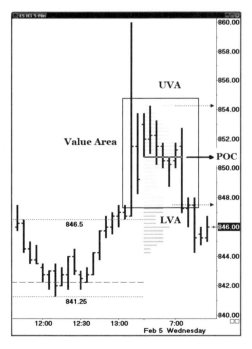

Figure 10.6   Intraday Trade Part 1. *Source:* S&P 500 Emini, 5-minute, CME, 2/5/03.

this example, neither occurred. The POC (2) remains unchanged and we exit half of our trade at this point. We then use the other end of the VA—the LVA (3) as our next target. Why? Because prices will explore both sides of the VA, using the POC as "home base."

The logic of this trading method is really quite simple. A range is established (Figure 10.10). The range has a time-weighted center which may or may not be its numerical mean. Prices will expand back and forth to the edges of the range, but will frequently return to the center. Prices may expand the range, but the center always pulls prices back.

11

THE CHIMPANZEE CROSS

The Chimpanzee Cross is so simple, that even a chimpanzee could trade it. The setup is also simple and elegant. It illustrates the advantages of using indicators from multiple time frames, in the same chart. You can trade this method on its own, or you can adapt it by changing the entry, target, and stop methods, or you can just use the underlying fundamentals of multiple time frame methods to create your own trading method.

It starts with a pair of moving averages on a short time frame chart. This example uses 5-period and 15-period moving averages on a 1-minute chart. Simply put, when the faster 5-period moving average crosses above the slower 15-period one, you take a long trade. When the 5-period crosses below 15-period, you take a short trade.

The reason you use two moving averages, rather than just watching prices above or below one moving average, is that two averages will help avoid choppy periods of horizontal price activity.

On a short time frame such as a one-minute chart, it is important to know what the overall trend is on a longer time frame. Remember the ubiquitous trading adage, "the trend is your friend." I like to watch the trend on a 13-minute chart. The simple way is to put up a 5- and 15-period moving average on a 13-minute chart, and only take short trades on the 1-minute chart when it is in agreement with the longer term trend of the 13-minute chart. But why have two charts? Why not just take the 5- and 15-minute moving averages from the 13-minute chart, and drop them into the 1-minute chart? That way I use less screen real estate, I have fewer charts to look at, and have all of the important information in one chart.

How to drop these longer time frame moving averages into a shorter time frame chart? Elementary, my dear Watson. Just use your elementary school math (Figure 11.1). A 5-period moving average on a 13-minute chart is exactly the same as a 65-period average on a 1-minute chart (5 periods × 13 minutes = 65 periods × 1 minute). Likewise, a 15-period moving average on a 13-minute chart is exactly the same as a 195-period moving average on a 1-minute chart (15 period × 13 minutes = 195 periods × 1 minute). So now in the 1-minute chart we have

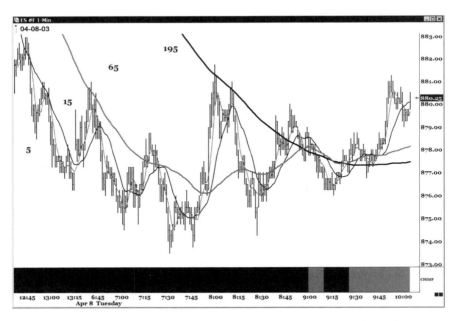

Figure 11.1 Multiple Time Frame Indicators. *Source:* S&P Emini, 1-minute, CME, 4/8/03.

two pairs of moving averages: 5 and 15, and 65 and 195. We use the longer term moving averages as a filter for the shorter term trades, as shown here.

I have also color coded a simple alert at the bottom of the chart to aid me visually: When the color band is black, the 65 is below the 195, the longer term trend is short and I only take short trades. When the color band is gray, the 65 is above the 195, the longer term trend is long, and I only take long trades.

Figure 11.2 zooms in on the short filter period on the left of this chart, to illustrate how the Chimpanzee Cross method works.

Arrows pointing to the right show short entries, and arrows pointing to the left show trade exits.

There are many different ways to trade the Chimpanzee Cross. In this example, you go short one tick below the low of

Figure 11.2   The Chimpanzee Cross. *Source:* S&P 500 Emini, 1-minute, CME, 4/8/03.

the first bar that occurs after the 5 crosses below the 15. Exit the trade one tick above the high of the first bar that occurs after the 5 crosses back above the 15. Trail the exit trigger; that is, if the next bar after that cross is lower than the previous, then use the high of that bar as a lower exit point. Sometimes, after the 5 crosses back above the 15, prices drop back down again until the 5 crosses back below the 15; by using a trailing exit trigger you would have stayed in the trade without exiting.

There are many other ways to enter and exit the Chimp. Can you think of some?

12

SHIFTED MOVING AVERAGES AND BOLLINGER BANDS

The moving averages—which include both stochastics and the moving average convergence divergence indicator (MACD)—are lagging indicators and, as such, are open to whipsaws. Whipsaws occur when prices jump back and forth across the moving average, and trigger false trade entry signals before the moving average can catch up with the price action. However the moving average may also function as a leading indicator when used together with the Bollinger Band. Both are lagging indicators, but by combining them together, they become leading indicators.

This application was introduced to me by Russell A. Lockhart, PhD., though I have adapted it to my own trading style. I would encourage you to do exactly the same—take a look, see how it works, and then adapt it for your own use.

Bollinger Bands, developed by John Bollinger, are moving averages of the standard deviation of prices, over a given period of time. *Standard deviation* (SDV) is the square root of the variance, and *variance* is a measure of how spread out a distribution is. These calculations are performed for you in the majority of charting programs. The Bollinger Bands show you exactly what price level, based on prices up and down over a given time period, would be considered to be out of the ordinary if prices were to then reach or exceed that level.

The default setting that John Bollinger uses is a 20-period moving average, set to 2-standard deviations. Statisticians recognize that 2-standard deviations is the normal level of deviation for the majority of charting applications. So the more volatile the swing in prices, the wider the bands are likely to be. Likewise, the smaller the swings in prices, the narrower those bands are likely to be.

One way to use this information is to observe what happens when the bands tighten. That is usually a sign that prices are consolidating in an increasingly narrow range, thus setting up for a major breakout from the established trading range. The bands themselves have limitations in that they are not leading indicators, although there are techniques for using the information they reveal to help make trading decisions. For instance, the point at which prices touch the band is often the signal of an impending reversal, which would then be confirmed by subsequent price action.

The way we combine the moving average and Bollinger Bands is to modify both of them in such a way that their crossing becomes significant. To do this, we emphasize what the Bollinger Bands tell us: First we increase the volatility beyond 2-standard deviations by pumping it up to 2.23, a Fibonacci number. Then we shorten the moving average from 20 down to 13, the sixth number in the Fibonacci sequence. Why use 13? Because it fits the method much better than 8 or 21. Of course, you can use a non-Fibonacci number such as 12, but be aware that 12 is the square root of 144, which is also a Fibonacci number!

Now let's modify the moving average by pulling it back three time periods. Why three? Because it is a moving average of the immediately preceding three time periods, and we want that average shifted back to the beginning of the preliminary time period. This is necessary because we are not interested in where the moving average touches prices, but where it touches the Bollinger Bands.

This setting aligns the shifted moving average (ShMA) correctly with the Extreme Bollinger Bands (EBB) so that when the ShMA crosses the EBB, it is a reliable signal for *exiting* the trade. Figure 12.1 shows the setup, with the indicated trade entry and exit points.

Candle (1) shows that the Bollinger Bands are narrowing; start to look for a major breakout of the trading range.

Candle (2) is a classic 123 reversal, with the entry point as shown. One candle *after* the entry, the ShMA crosses above the EBB. (It may look as if the ShMA crossed before trade entry, but remember we have shifted it back three candles, so that the point at which it actually crosses the band is three candles to the right.) At this point—when the ShMA crosses the EBB— you might decide to forgo the Fibonacci Growth Wave target and instead exit at the cross.

Candle (3) indicates the point where the ShMA crossed the upper EBB signifying the point to exit the trade.

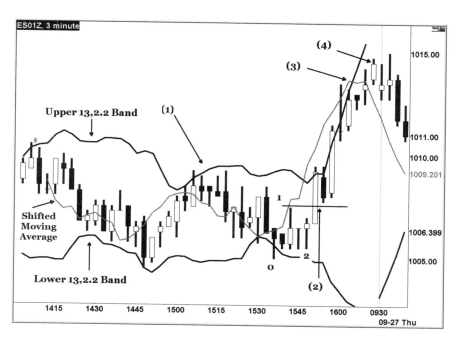

Figure 12.1 Shifted Moving Averages and Bollingers. *Source:* S&P Emini, 3-minute, CME, 9/26/01.

Candle (4) shows where the cross actually takes place—near the apex of the trade. Notice how this would have given you a much more profitable trade than simply exiting at the W3 target of 1.62, or exiting when prices touched the upper band.

You can use this method with any of your normal trade entry techniques. It only becomes significant when the ShMA moves outside of the EBB, and then it is only useful as a signal to exit the trade. But when used in this manner, it can provide you with the ability to better pick the likely top of a price trend. Figure 12.2 shows an example of using the ShMA/EBB method to exit a trade on the Chimpanzee Cross.

(1) 5 EMA crosses above the 15 EMA. (Note that 65 EMA is above the 195 EMA, so we would look for long trades.)

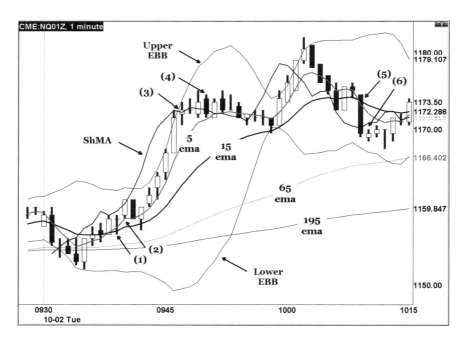

Figure 12.2 Using ShMA/EBB to Exit a Chimpanzee Cross Trade. *Source:* Nasdaq Emini, 1-minute, CME, 10/02/01.

(2) Trade executes long one tick above the high of the previous candle (1) 1159.5.

(3) SHMA crosses the EBB . . .

(4) . . . at this point (remember it has been pulled back three candles). So the trade exits one tick below the low of this candle, 1171, for a gain of 10.5 points on the Nasdaq E-mini.

(5) The 5 EMA crosses back down below the 15 EMA after this candle has printed, so the traditional exit using the Chimpanzee Cross method would be one tick below this candle.

(6) Trade exits during the candle at 1168.5, for a gain of 9 points. In this example, the SHMA/EBB gave us a better exit.

Again, it is important to observe and compare the different methods to see if one has a clear advantage over the other, based on which financial instrument you are trading and on which time period.

13

CITIZEN'S ENVELOPE

This is a simple, yet effective technique that I learned from Citizen. It involves two moving averages of the same length to create an envelope: a 3-period, exponential moving average (EMA) shifted forward three periods, and a 3-period EMA shifted back three periods. It can also be used with the ShMA/EBB method from Chapter 12 or, for that matter, with the Chimpanzee Cross method from Chapter 11.

The forward 3 EMA (3 EMA +3) is your entry trigger. The back 3 EMA (3 EMA – 3), since it is shifted back, is too late to give you a signal, but it confirms whether or not you are in a trend and, together with the forward EMA, creates the envelope in which prices should be moving. The advantage to the combination of a backward-looking and a forward-looking indicator is twofold. First, it creates a support and resistance range, which we refer to as the *envelope,* based partially on the look back. Second, it provides a confirmation about the trend itself, and this is essential to effective interpretation. With all forms of charting and, for that matter, technical analysis in a broader sense, interpretation is the difficult part. We can look back and confidently demonstrate what took place because we have a range of information that has already occurred. However, in the minute-to-minute analysis of rapidly moving prices, we have more difficulty determining precisely where we are in the trend. Are we at the beginning, the middle, or the end? It is quite easy to misread the signals and to draw the wrong conclusion. What might look like a significant signal today could, in fact, be a much larger counter-movement in a much bigger trend. The current, developing chart is a tree in a vast and complex forest; the Citizen's Envelope enables us to rise above the fray and take a broader look at the emerging trend.

The Citizen's Envelope, your broader look at the trend, works best on a one-minute chart. As always, use a higher time frame, or slower moving averages within the given time frames, to confirm the longer-term trend.

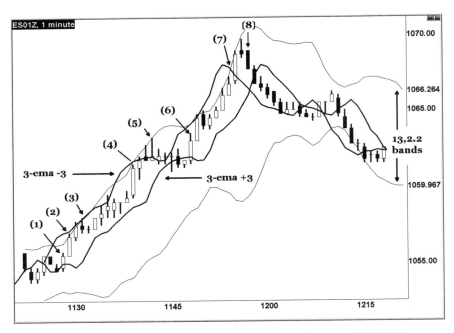

Figure 13.1 Citizen's Envelope with the ShMA/EBB. *Source:* S&P Emini, 1-minute, CME, 10/3/01.

Figure 13.1 shows the envelope, as well as the Extreme Bollinger Bands (EBB) from Chapter 12:

(1) Aggressive long entry is when the first up candle closes above the 3 EMA +3 line.

(2) A safer entry is the candle after that, which has trended above the 3 EMA +3 line.

(3) This is a reversal point. If you do some back-testing on other charts, you will see there is often a pause after the first three up candles in this pattern. You can see that congestion pause on this chart at candle (3) and the one after it.

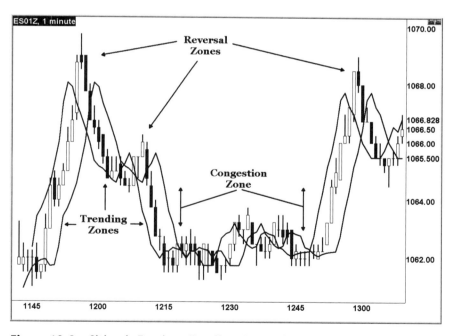

Figure 13.2 Citizen's Envelope Trending, Reversal, and Congestion Zones.
Source: S&P Emini, 1-minute, CME, 10/03/01.

(4) Exit when the ShMA crosses the EBB, as shown here and in Chapter 12.

(5) The actual exit occurs at this candle.

(6) The strength of these combined methods is clearly shown here as the cross of the ShMA into the EBB will simultaneously close the Citizen's envelope. Here, the envelope did not quite close all the way, so we take the next long entry as shown at candle (6).

(7) Again, exit is triggered at the cross point as shown here, with actual exit occurring at candle (8).

From Figure 13.2, you can see how Citizen's Envelope can be used to help identify reversals and congestion zones.

Citizen's Envelope alone cannot pinpoint a congestion zone before or even during the beginning of such a zone, but there are many other ways to tell as described in Chapter 3. Refer to Figures 3.8, 3.9, and 3.10.

14

GANN ANGLES

This chapter introduces a basic method for making short-term price predictions based on a results-oriented treatment of the relation between price and time. This approach is based on the theories of W. D. Gann, as interpreted by Russell A. Lockhart, PhD. It does not purport to represent the teachings of either; rather, it shows my own practical applications of those teachings.

Although Gann Angles are not predictive in isolation, when used together with the basic Fibonacci techniques from Part One of this book, they can help steer you clear of bad trades and keep you in the good ones.

SQUARE OF TIME

Draw a square using time as the horizontal x-axis and price as the vertical y-axis—the same axes that you have on your charting software (Figure 14.1). Then apply angles to those squares, the most important of which is the 45-degree angle, which is the midpoint between the horizontal (0 degree) and vertical (90 degree) axes. Just as the 45-degree angle is halfway between "flat" and "straight up," so 50% is halfway between the top and bottom of a trading range.

Price-time squares can be drawn between any two important prices (your Y axis) and any two important times (your X

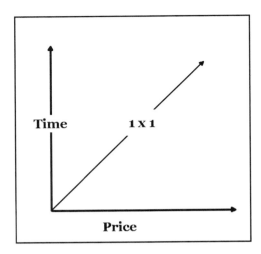

Figure 14.1   The Price/Time Square.

axis). It is up to you to determine which prices and which times to use.

I like to use the first 30-minute period of the trading day, from 9:30 to 10:00 Eastern Standard Time (EST). During that opening half-hour, which accounts for 15% of the trading day's time, up to 50% of the day's volume is traded. Also, during that period, the initial trading ranges for the day may become firmly established and those initial trading ranges become fractal seeds for the rest of the day.

The X axis is divided into 30-minute increments. On the 30-minute chart in Figure 14.2, I have drawn vertical lines at each 30-minute increment for the trading day. Setting that chart aside for a moment, Figure 14.3 shows lines drawn on the Y axis. Increments are the high and the low of that first 30-minute period. Let's say the high was 1102, and the low was 1098. That represents an increment of 4 points. If you have a retracement tool in your charting system, you can draw the four-point increments easily in one quick tracing, using multiples of 100%, as shown. If not, you can calculate them in a spreadsheet and then

Figure 14.2 30-minute Time Increments. *Source:* S&P Emini, 30-minute, CME, 9/17/01.

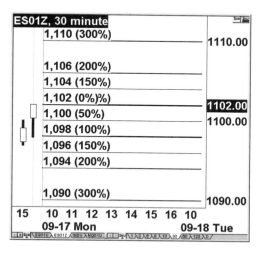

Figure 14.3 Price Increments Based on First 30-minute Range. *Source:* S&P Emini, 30-minute, CME, 9/17/01.

draw each horizontal line manually. I've drawn the lines in Figure 14.3, where you will see 1102 has a value of 0% and 1098 has a value of 100%.

Putting the two sets of drawing together, we end up with Figure 14.4, which now gives us perfect squares from which to draw 45-degree angles and the subangles within.

To apply this technique to a specific trade example, look at the opening of the S&P E-mini futures on Monday, September 17, 2001, the first day of trading after the terrorist attacks on New York and Washington (Figure 14.5). First I draw vertical lines every 30 minutes. Then I zoom in on a 1-minute chart and wait for the first half hour to pass (9:30 to 10:00 A.M.) so that I can draw in my horizontal lines.

Since the range of the initial 30-minutes was 1034.5 – 1018.5 or 16 points, each box size will be 16 points high. Thus, the second box up, where the retracement line reads 200%, is 1050.5. I also draw half boxes to represent a 50% retracement, which is the most important retracement level.

Figure 14.4 Time/Price Squares. *Source:* S&P Emini, 30-minute, CME, 9/17/01.

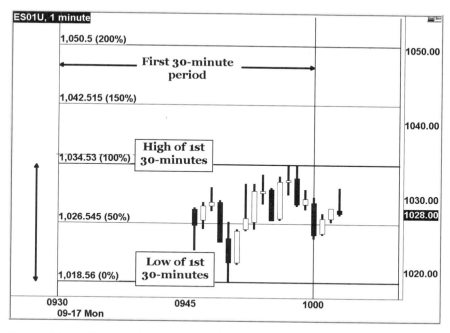

Figure 14.5   Gann Angles—Drawing the First Half-Hour. *Source:* S&P Emini, 1-minute, CME, 9/17/01.

Figure 14.6 is a 2-minute chart of the same period, which converts the boxes to squares. This enables you to see the 1×1 angle as 45 degrees. The chart also shows the three most important angles in the price-time square: 1×1, 1×2, and 2×1. To draw them, you simply anchor one end of your ray line at 0 and the other end at the 1×1, 1×2, and 2×1 points (intersections) shown.

Figure 14.6 shows lines drawn down from the MSH. That assumes that the 0 point is the MSH and that we are looking for angles down from the open. But you can also draw up from the MSL, as shown in the next chart, Figure 14.7.

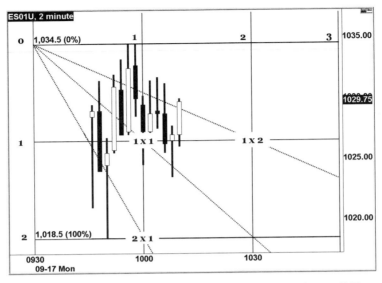

Figure 14.6   Primary Gann Angles. *Source:* S&P Emini, 2-minute, CME, 9/17/01.

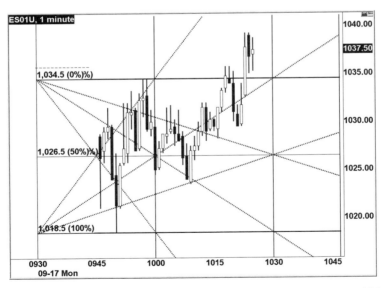

Figure 14.7   Primary Gann Angles Drawn Both Up and Down. *Source:* S&P Emini, 1-minute, CME, 9/17/01.

As time passes, we look for a pattern to emerge. Some prices
start to hug the 1 × 1 up line, but the pattern is not really clear.
Notice that the futures market did not open until 9:45 on this
particular day, because of an overnight gap which resulted in a
mandatory price lock for fifteen minutes. So perhaps we should
redraw our 30-minute vertical lines from 9:45, rather than 9:30.

Figure 14.8 shows how all the pieces fit together, like a puz-
zle, simply by shifting our start to 9:45. Note how prices initially
followed the 1 × 2 line down. That does not guarantee prices will
stay down, far from it. But these two laws of price-time squares
become self-evident:

1. Trending prices tend to follow the slope of a prime price/
   time angle until they tire of that slope.

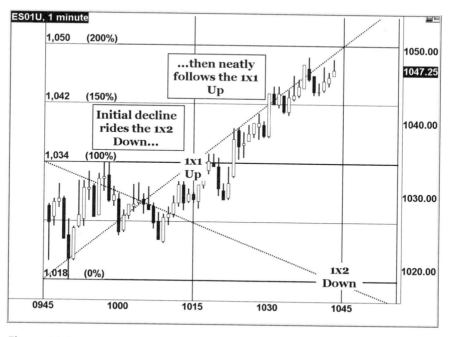

Figure 14.8 Repositioned Angles. *Source:* S&P Emini, 1-minute, CME, 9/17/01.

2. Once prices leave a particular angle, they will automatically seek out or tend toward creation of another nearby angle pattern, either in the same direction or in a reversal direction.

After prices broke above the 1×2 down support, they latched onto the next major up escalator, the 1×1, which is the most powerful one. And up they rode, the 1×1 acting simultaneously as price attractor and as resistance, for the next hour. Now let's look at what happens when prices can no longer keep up the steep rate of ascent that the 1×1 demands.

As shown in Figure 14.9, when prices can no longer keep up their steep rate of ascent, but still want to go up, they will tend

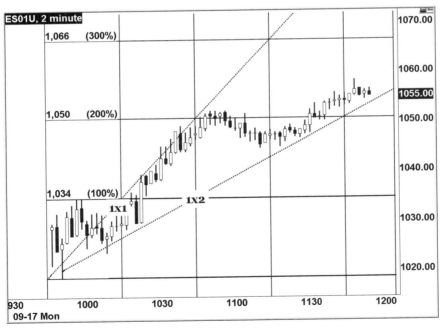

Figure 14.9 Seeking the Next Angle. *Source:* S&P Emini, 2-minute, CME, 9/17/01.

to look for the next important angle, the 1 × 2. September 17, 2001, was a very volatile, high-volume day. Such days tend to be the best trading days for measuring the emotions of the trading public through any method that uses mathematics.

One problem with this particular technique is that the further prices move from the 0 point—in this example, from 9:45 A.M.—the smaller the angles. So you would find yourself looking for 1 × 3 angles to ride, then 1 × 4, and so on. In my experience, using the 30-minute price-time square, two to three hours is the maximum period that you would want to use the lines. You then want to start looking for another important price point from which to anchor a new set of Gann Angles. Usually this is a major intraday MSL or MSH. It is especially desirable if, as in this example, that MSH occurs right at one of the 30-minute time increments, so that you do not have to redraw all those lines. Usually this is the case.

At 11:45—after exactly two hours—prices formed a major MSH which ended up being the high of the day. I redrew the lines and rode them down.

Every single major MSH and MSL for the rest of the day turned at one of the four Gann Angles that I drew. And several of the major price trends also followed the price-time slope of those same lines. You will also note that several price trends fell between the lines, and this is quite common. As I pointed out above, when prices leave one Gann Angle, they will instinctively seek out the next one. That is precisely what you see happening here in Figure 14.10. I have marked the critical turning points with arrows.

Skeptics may argue that if you draw enough lines, prices are bound to "appear" to follow their slope or turn at their time intersections. If you are one of these, try shifting those lines away by a few points or by 15 minutes, as we did in Figure 14.6. The proof of the pudding is in the eating!

The price-time angles provide another overlay on my trading road map. I always keep an eye on it. If I am in an open position

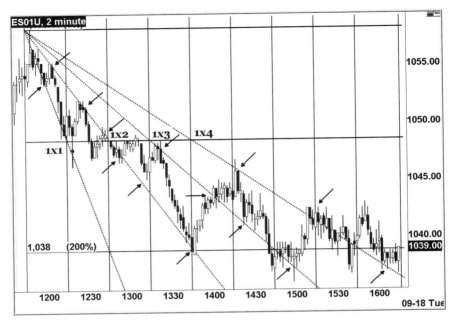

Figure 14.10   Gann Angle Turning Points. *Source:* S&P Emini, 2-minute, CME, 9/17/01.

and I see that prices have jumped tracks from one Gann Angle and are headed for the next, I will have an even better idea of where I should exit. And if the Fibonacci wave or retracement targets line up—as is usually the case—then I have just received a double confirmation.

Such double confirmations are highly desirable, because they increase our chances of being right. Just as the Dow Theory is based on the premise that independent confirmation is essential before any conclusions can be drawn, the same is true for this theory and any other math-based approach to analysis. At the same time, we also need to accept the fact that there is going to be a degree of random movement in any price structure; so while this approach can improve our short-term forecasting, it is not foolproof. Nothing is. Remember, prices do not have individual consciousness (even though it might appear that they do) but are representations of the supply and demand factors of thousands of traders, all interacting at the same time in an auction marketplace. We have to expect a high level of chaos in this environment, even if we can identify predictive patterns that emerge from within that chaos.

PART FOUR

BUILDING GOOD
TRADING HABITS

It is easy to get confused when the market is moving in so many directions and generating so many signals. You see what you believe to be an excellent long set-up, so you press the button and enter a trade. But no sooner have you done so, then you find a plethora of signals that all indicate short rather than long would have been the sensible decision. Prices drop, and you hit the exit button, losing $100. No sooner have you done that, then the trade moves back in your favor. If you had stayed in the trade, you would be up $500. You might compound the mistake by jumping back in the trade, usually at the point where prices have reached exhaustion and rapidly drop back down. What did you do wrong? Why are you buying high and selling low instead of the opposite?

The answer: You listened to too many voices. It is important to develop a set of familiar and clearly defined trading methods and tools, and to stick to those. Of course that does not mean that you should trade them day in and day out, nor that you should use those methods without adapting them as the nature of the market itself changes—as surely it does. Most successful traders will agree on three key laws of successful trading:

1. *Methodology:* Develop a simple, clear method or set of methods that works for you.

2. *Re-examine:* Employ a simple, clear set of filters that tell you when to use those methods, and when not to.

3. *Change:* Constantly upgrade and update your methods and filters through relentless study, observation, and testing.

The first three parts of this book introduced many techniques as building blocks for a simple, clear method for trading. Part Four deals with the hard part: developing good trading habits that extend beyond the hours of the trading day to pre- and posttrade analysis. This in itself requires a three-part system:

1. Carta Diem
2. Trade Logs
3. Filters

Carta Diem is a specific set of charts that I put on my web site at the end of each trading day that helps me to review what happened during the day, and to forecast what is likely to happen the following day. It gives me a clear snapshot of the current trend, likely highs and lows and even the likely support and resistance points along the way. As you would expect, much of it is Fibonacci based. Some of it is not.

The Trade log is a spreadsheet where I meticulously log every single trade that I take, as well as hundred of trades that I do NOT take.

Filters are how I decide whether to trade or not to trade.

Like an important business meeting when just getting the people together at the table is going to create results, so developing the habit of creating these three steps delivers the required result: Building better trading habits.

15

CARTA DIEM: "SEIZE THE CHART!"

Each morning I mark my charts with critical information that has been supplied to me by the price action from the day before. This information helps me to fine-tune my Fibonacci targets, and to determine the important price points for entering and exiting trades. I provide these marked charts each morning to subscribers of my web site but you can do it yourself if you have half an hour to spare before the market opens. Hopefully, you will already be familiar with everything you see in this chapter, from previous chapters of this book. I have also included some examples of how I use this information during the trading day.

Carta Diem is made up of these sections:

1. *Daily and Weekly Charts* show longer term patterns and targets.

2. *Reports* for the week. I set alarms for 25-minutes before all major scheduled economic reports. I do not recommend trades immediately prior to scheduled reports.

3. *Overnight Activity* charts show overnight highs and lows. These are always important pivots during the day, even

after they have been broken. I also look at the 50% range pivot and the overnight POC, particularly in reference to the previous day's POC.

4. *Price Histogram:* I mark the previous day's POC as the major pivot for the upcoming day and the other days' POC above and below that as the Natural Trading Range (NTR) for the day.

5. *Fibonacci Corner:* I mark the Fibonacci retracements and wave targets as shown; these are always excellent pivots during the next day.

6. *Regression Channel:* Watch the channel carefully for intraday breakouts. Use it also to predict reversal points.

DAILY AND WEEKLY CHARTS

Figure 15.1 shows a typical daily chart with wave targets and regression channels drawn in. I will use whatever drawing tools I feel are relevant to give me a good road-map of that particular chart. Here you can see the W3 target zone of 1.38–1.62 drawn on the initial seed wave.

Some regression channel indicators will show not only the standard deviation lines (a), but also percent deviation lines (b). This is handy because once the regression channel is drawn from the beginning of the seed wave to (c), sometimes prices form critical peaks above and below the two standard deviation lines. These peaks can become important support and resistance points, which in turn become important channel lines. The percent deviation lines (b) can then be manually "fit" to those points, as this one was to the top of the seed wave.

Finally, note that W3 registered at point (d).

Weekly candles show the same data as Daily candles, but go further back in time (Figure 15.2). Quite often the weekly candles give quite a different picture than the daily, as is the case

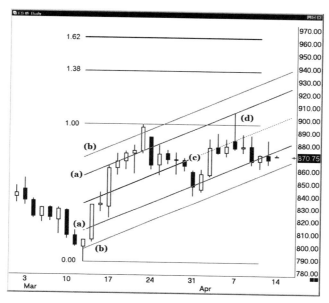

Figure 15.1 Daily Chart. *Source:* S&P Emini, Daily, CME, March–April 2003.

Figure 15.2 Weekly Chart. *Source:* S&P500 Index, Weekly, 2001–2003.

here. The trend lines show obvious trends converging, and the price histogram POC is noted here because it acts as a strong price attractor as well as resistance point.

REPORTS

I do not trade the news. I do not like the way that prices are manipulated as time approaches a scheduled news release, and I do not like the way that prices whipsaw around in knee-jerk reactions immediately after a scheduled news release or economic report. The reason for this is that the natural trading indicators that I use to help me trade are rendered temporarily meaningless in a highly manipulated and emotional environment. I do, however, trade the second reaction to a news release; this is almost always strong. It could be a continuation of the original knee-jerk move, or it could be the market coming to its senses and reversing back from that knee-jerk move. Either way, once the market had tipped its hand following a news release, the indicators will begin to make sense again.

For this reason, I take note of the scheduled news releases each day. Some charting programs allow you to mark them on your charts (using a vertical line placed at the time point); others allow you to create a time-triggered sound or pop-up alert. Either way, I stop trading 15 minutes before a scheduled news release, and resume trading after the first market response to that release.

There are many sources of information online. One handy source is Yahoo! Finance. Their URL is http://biz.yahoo.com /c/e.html. It contains hot links to the specific news source from Briefing.com—their direct URL is http://www.briefing.com—so that you can get more detail on the information if necessary. I generally ignore scheduled Earning Reports because the earnings reporting season extends for at least one month, four times a year, and during its peak, several companies will be reporting each day; the important ones normally report after market hours anyhow.

OVERNIGHT TRADING ACTIVITY

With the larger picture of the daily and weekly trends in hand, I then take a look at what happened in the futures market overnight (Figure 15.3). For this purpose, constant tick charts are more useful and give a better picture by compressing the

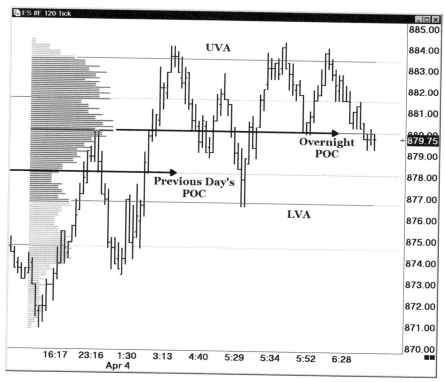

Figure 15.3   Overnight Trading Activity. *Source:* S&P Emini, 120-tick, CME, 4/10/03.

entire 17-hour session into bars that are determined by the number of trades, not time. Constant tick charts are explained in more detail in Chapter 17.

I am looking for four important elements: (1) The overall size of the overnight trading range, (2) the amount of the gap between the previous day's close at 4:15 P.M. and today's open at 9:30 A.M., (3) the POC for the overnight session (and its relative location compared to the previous day's POC), and (4) whether any significant Fibonacci seeds were planted during the overnight session. Also, a Fibonacci wave that began during the previous afternoon

Figure 15.4 Using Overnight Pivots for Daytime Trades. *Source:* S&P Emini, 360-tick, CME, 11/18/02.

might actually reach its target during the overnight session and then begin a retrace into the next day's morning session. It is very helpful to have this information, gleaned from the 24-hour constant tick chart shown in Figure 15.3.

Figure 15.4 shows price action that began the night before, and how that can be carried over into the trading day. Times shown at the bottom of the chart are Pacific Time, so the day session opened at 6:30 A.M. Pacific time.

The initial overnight support line (913.25) is shown. At point (a), prices dropped below that line for the first time. This

Figure 15.5 Applying Fibonacci to Those Trades. *Source:* S&P Emini, 360-tick, CME, 11/18/02.

was our first indication that we should be looking short. That was confirmed at point (b), when exactly the same line converted from previous support and became the new resistance level. Remember, support acts as support until it fails; it then become resistance. Prices rallied back up a second time, and reversed at exactly the same resistance point (c). After failing to break that resistance point, prices then dropped toward the next obvious line, the overnight low at (d), where they found support after touching through twice and forming a double bottom MSL at (e). The reversal back to the upside was confirmed by the 123 pattern shown.

As Figure 15.4 shows, being aware of the overnight price action can be very important for the next day. Figure 15.5 shows how we could have integrated our knowledge of Fibonacci into making actual trades.

When prices broke through the initial support line 913.25, the first seed wave (1) was created. It then entered into a retracement wave (2) up to 0.38 as shown, turning around at the overnight support line. This turnaround was our signal to enter the short for W3, which we rode down into the W3 Zone, exiting below 908 (3). Retracement wave (4) failed at the same overnight support line, indicating that there may be a W5 extension. After dropping back into the W3 zone and consolidating there—recall that W5 extensions are often complex—prices finally dropped and hit the W5 target just below the overnight low. The combination of hitting the overnight low and hitting the W5 target of 2.26 × the initial seed wave, was a strong indication that we would see a reversal back to the upside, as confirmed by the 123 reversal pattern that you can see at the end of the chart.

Figure 15.6 shows that the 123 long reversal was also tradable as soon as the reversal seed wave (1) was in place. We simply use our knowledge of Fibonacci to target the potential W3 as shown.

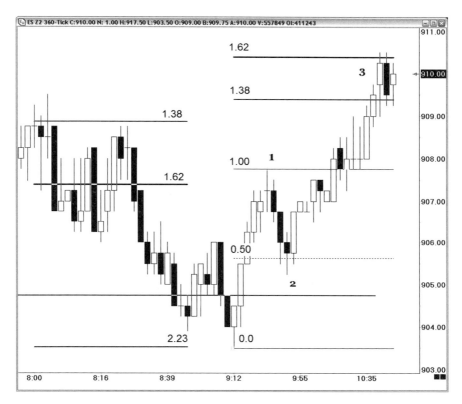

Figure 15.6   Trading the Reversal. *Source:* S&P Emini, 360-tick, CME, 11/18/02.

PRICE HISTOGRAM

The basics of the price histogram are covered in Chapter 10. However there are other uses of the price histogram chart. One is to give me an idea of where the trading range is likely to be for the next day. I call this the Natural Trading Range (NTR). It is not a prediction, only a suggestion of where prices will *naturally* range between given previous price activity and the centers of gravity formed by the points of control from previous days. Remember that the price histogram's POC is just the price point where the market spent the most amount of time on a given day.

Figure 15.7 shows how I estimate the NTR for the next day. Because the POC has a strong "gravitational pull" of its own—after all, it is where prices spent the most amount of time trading yesterday—there is a high probability that prices will return to the previous day's POC *at some point during the trading* day.

Armed with this knowledge, the previous day's POC will most likely act as one of the extremes of the next day's trading range. If that POC is too close to the current one, I will look

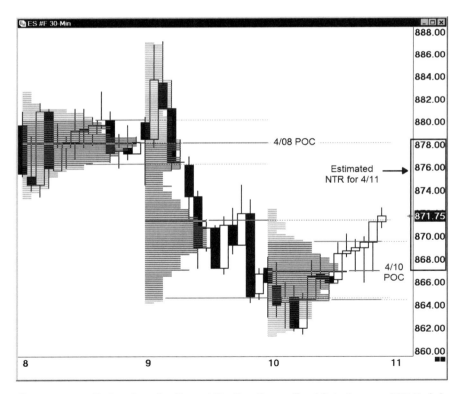

Figure 15.7 Estimating the Natural Trading Range for 4/11. *Source:* S&P Emini, 30-minute, CME, 4/08–4/10/03.

back for the next obvious POC, then look at prices on the Overnight Trading Activity chart to see where prices are likely to open the next morning. In Figure 15.7, prices closed above the 4/10 POC and then on the overnight chart I saw that prices were gapping up even further. This told me that the 4/08 POC would be the likely high of the Natural Trading Range for 4/11, barring any unforeseen news. Because prices were already so far above the POC of 4/10, I simply used that as the estimated NTR low, giving me a range of 867–878.

Figure 15.8 shows what happened on the next day. The actual trading range ended up as 865–884.

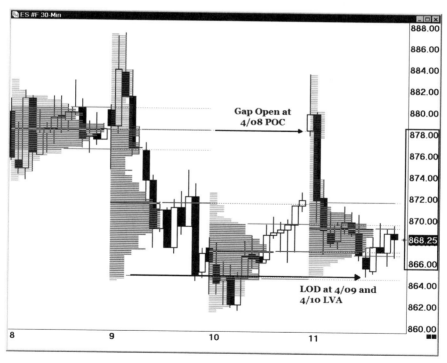

Figure 15.8 Actual Trading Range for 4/11. *Source:* S&P Emini, 30-minute, CME, 4/08–4/10/03.

How can you use this knowledge in your trading? If you are in a long position and prices are approaching the NTR high (in this case, 878) then that is a good place to exit the long position or at least to start tightening your stop. If prices then move back down and drop below the lower value area from that same day (in this case, 876) then that is a good indication to enter a short position. Of course, you should use other indicators to confirm the trade. Having entered that short at or around 876, you would then exit the short as close to the lower end of the estimated NTR as possible.

FIBONACCI CORNER

This is where I mark the major Fibonacci-based seed wave targets and retracement pivots. The important thing to remember about Fibonacci is that you can apply it to whatever trading method you are using, even if you are not trading seed waves on their own merit. Being aware of the wave targets will always give you a better exit point for whatever method you are using to trade. Both Fibonacci and overnight support points to trade levels for the next day. The same principal follows by looking at the previous day's (daytime) Fibonacci points. Figure 15.9 shows how I mark the chart at the end of the day. At the close of November 21, 2002, there were two possibilities for price action on the next day: either prices would retrace, or there would be a new third wave up. There was no way to know which way prices would go so I drew both retracement pivots, and the W3 targets, as shown. If prices dropped, they would likely drop to the 50% pivot. If prices continued up, they would probably extend to the W3 zone located between 138.2% and 161.8% of the initial seed wave, as shown.

Figure 15.10 shows what actually happened, and how the W3 zone was a natural place to take profits on longs.

Figure 15.9 Up or Down? *Source:* S&P Emini, 30-minute, CME, 11/19–11/20/02.

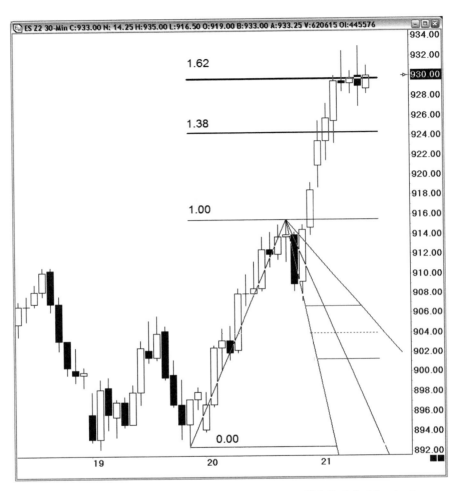

Figure 15.10   Fibonacci Corner Seed Wave. *Source:* S&P Emini, 30-minute, CME, 11/19–11/21/02.

REGRESSION CHANNEL

The 1000-tick chart (Figure 15.11) is useful because it allows you to look back at several days worth of 24-hour tick data, without the plethora of bars that you would have with a shorter tick count. I use a regression channel on this chart to show me both the overall direction, and the bounds of the major trading ranges. Recall from Chapter 6 that a major trend can be tracked using the regression channel tool (available on most charting programs) by anchoring it to the first two high or low points in a new trend.

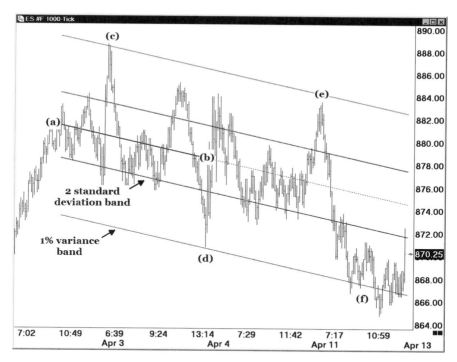

Figure 15.11 1000-Tick Regression Channel. *Source:* S&P Emini, 1000-tick, CME, 4/3–4/11/03.

The initial regression line was drawn from (a) to (b), and projects onward from there. Point (a) was the beginning of the downtrend, and point (b) was the major bottom (d). The 2-standard deviation bands then automatically draw a channel in which 95% of prices are bound. I then manually added a percent deviation band to the channel, so that the band would stretch up to touch (c). This amounted to 1% deviation, but the amount of deviation is inconsequential. What is interesting is that once the % deviation band is matched to (c), notice how the other key reversal points (d), (e), and (f) also match the same band!

As part of Carta Diem, I do not use this 1000-tick chart specifically to trade from, though I will use it to help fine-tune trade exits and to help tell me when a trend is about to reverse.

16

THE TRADE LOG AND BUILDING FILTERS

Maintaining a trade log is the single most important part of your trading arsenal. Apparently it is also the most overlooked as well, because most traders I talk to do not keep a log. To me, it is more important than any single technical indicator or pattern that I have ever learned. It has saved me countless times and I will illustrate how it can help you.

I keep a log of every trade that I make. In addition, I keep a log of every trade that I do *not* make. The log is in a spreadsheet and contains all of the basic information for each trade: date, entry time, entry price, exit time, and exit price. It also contains a series of information columns that I later use to determine how I should best filter my trading methods. These include the chronological trade order of the morning (1, 2, 3, etc.), the overall trend, the volume of the previous 3-minute bar, the wiggle (lowest point in the trade), the highest price reached in the trade, and the reason for the exit, which I have categorized into about a dozen sortable shortcut names. I also enter a shorthand name of the trade system or method and the targets and stops for all contracts in the trade. I typically trade multiples of two contracts and so will have separate targets for the two. I also jot down the reason for the targets.

This may seem like a lot of work but it only takes about 15 seconds to input all of the information for any one trade. Like anything, when it becomes habit, it becomes second nature. I input the information without even thinking.

A working sample of the trade log spreadsheet that I use can be downloaded from www.enthios.com (Figure 16.1).

Periodically, I analyze the information in the trade log by sorting the different columns and applying filters to determine where the most and least profitable trades are located. For example, when I was first developing the EN method described in Chapter 17, I realized that it was not profitable during the middle of the day. After I had completed several hundred trades, I filtered all of the trades by time of day to see if there were any particular periods where the method just did not work well. As it turned out, the method was very profitable between 9:30 and 10:30 A.M., and from 2:00 P.M. to 3:45 P.M. In-between, it was only moderately profitable. To conserve mental energy and to minimize risk, I stopped trading the method between 10:30 and 2:00. However, I did continue to paper trade it during the off peak hours, in order to maintain a benchmark of data against which to compare future market tendencies.

I then began to notice that at times there were great trades to be made after 10:30; other times, it seemed as if the entire morning was just dead. It seemed obvious that volume had something to do with it, so I began to keep track of volume. I selected a rudimentary way of tracking this feature: I wrote down the volume of the 3-minute bar immediately preceding the bar in which the trade occurred. Very quickly I discovered that if the volume (for the S&P Futures Emini) was under 3,000 contracts, the efficiency of the trades dropped off. I also realized that when the 3-minute volume stayed consistently above 3,000 contracts even after 10:30 A.M., the trade efficiency continued beyond 10:30. Knowing that this was just a rudimentary filter at best, I came up with an equally rudimentary application of the filter: I decided to trade in the morning until 10:30 and, thereafter,

Figure 16.1 Trade Log.

																						MTD # Trades		
																						MTD P&L		
Days								Filters														Current # Trades		20
21-Nov																						Current P&L		$1,021
21-Nov																								

= current month cumulative
= current time period

Date	Day	Entry Time	b/s	Type	Entry	Seq	S x2	Sw x1	V	Wiggle	Trade Max	T1	Stop	C1	T2	Stop	IB Exit	C2	C2 Exit Rea	Exit	Time	C1 (21 / 15.00)	C2 (20 / 10.25)	$ (20 / $1,021)
21-Nov	Thu	9:30	l	MC	921.75							927.3		927.3				929.75		15:30	6:00	5.50	8.00	665.40
21-Nov	Thu	9:35	l	SX	922						933	928	924	932				928.25		12:10	2:35	10.00	6.25	802.90
21-Nov	Thu	9:42	l	EN	923.25	1	y	y	13		923.5			921.8				921.75	MB	9:46	0:04	(1.50)	(1.50)	(159.60)
21-Nov	Thu	9:50	l	EN	923.75	2	y	y	9	922.75	925.5			924.8				923.5	IB	9:59	0:09	1.00	(0.25)	27.90
21-Nov	Thu	10:00	l	EN	925.25	3	y	y	14	925	927.3			926.3				923.5	MB	10:00	0:00	1.00	(1.75)	(47.10)
21-Nov	Thu	10:08	s	cEN	922.5	4	n	n	14		921.5			921.5				923.25	IB	10:16	0:08	1.00	(0.75)	2.90
21-Nov	Thu	10:21	l	cEN	924	5	n	n	8.8	922.5	926.3			925				926	PH	10:29	0:08	1.00	2.00	140.40
21-Nov	Thu	10:28	s	EN	923.5	6	n	n	12		923.3			925.3				925.25	MB	10:45	0:17	(1.75)	(1.75)	(184.60)
21-Nov	Thu	10:45	l	EN	926.25	7	n	y	9	925.25				927.3				929	LP162°	10:55	0:10	1.00	2.75	177.90
21-Nov	Thu	13:20	l	SX	932.25									931.5				931.5		14:10	0:50	(0.75)	(0.75)	(84.60)
21-Nov	Thu	14:12	l	EN	934		n	y	4.6		934.3			932.3				932.25	MB	14:14	0:02	(1.75)	(1.75)	(184.60)
21-Nov	Thu	14:15	s	EN	931.5		n	y	5	932.25				930.5			930.5	929.75	W3	14:20	0:05	1.00	1.75	127.90
21-Nov	Thu	14:20	s	SX	929.25									931.5				931.5		14:30	0:10	(2.25)	(2.25)	(234.60)
21-Nov	Thu	14:36	l	EN	931.5		n	n	4.8	930.25				932.5				933	IB	14:51	0:15	1.00	1.50	115.40
21-Nov	Thu	14:52	l	cEN	934.25		n	y	7.7	933.5	936.3			935.3				934.5	IB	14:59	0:07	1.00	0.25	52.90
21-Nov	Thu	14:55	l	SX	935.75									932.5				932.5		15:10	0:15	(3.25)	(3.25)	(334.60)
21-Nov	Thu	15:03	s	EN	932.75		n	n	7.8	933.75	931.3			931.8				932.75	IB	15:16	0:13	1.00	0.00	40.40
21-Nov	Thu	15:19	l	EN	934		n	y	10	933.52	935.3			935	931			930	W3	15:29	0:03	1.00	2.00	140.40
21-Nov	Thu	15:26	s	EN	932		n	n	13	932.5	928.3			930	930			930	MB	15:44	0:07	(1.25)	(1.25)	(134.60)
21-Nov	Thu	15:45	l	cEN	931.25		n	n	9.7	930.5	933.3			932.5				932.5	IB	15:56	0:11	1.00	1.00	90.40

Table 16.1 Effects of Trade Sequence during the Day,
April–November 2002

Trade Sequence in Day	No. of Trades Recorded	Profit after Commission ($)	Successful Trades (%)
1	140	2,881	60
2	141	3,484	66
3	140	5,051	65

until the first 3-minute volume bar that dropped below 3,000. At that point, I would stop trading for the rest of the morning. That might occur at 10:30 or it might occur at noon. I would then wait until 2:00 P.M. After 2:00 P.M., I would not start trading again until the first volume bar that rose above 3,000. That would be my trigger to start trading the afternoon session.

I also noticed that the first trade of the day often turned out to be a bad one. By evaluating trade sequences, I was able to reconfirm this, as shown in Table 16.1.

Knowing that the market changes its dynamics continuously, I decided to study a more recent section of the market, starting in August when the Bear market began to turn into a Bull market. The "First trade = Bad trade" syndrome was much more pronounced, as shown in Table 16.2.

Of course, Tables 16.1 and 16.2 show all EN trades, not those that are filtered by time, volume, and trend (more on these

Table 16.2 Trade Sequences, August–November 2002

Trade Sequence in Day	No. of Trades Recorded	Profit after Commission ($)	Successful Trades (%)
1	76	−1,105	53
2	76	458	63
3	74	1,502	64

shortly). Table 16.3 shows the same sequences over the same period, but looking at filtered trades only.

Table 16.3 confirmed two important points: First, the filters improved profitability and efficiency while reducing the number of trades; second, the first trade of the day still was not a good one. Comparing Tables 16.2 and 16.3 confirmed another important point: The market is dynamic, and it pays to constantly update your trading method and the filters that you apply in order to help minimize the low percentage trade outcomes.

I had determined that volume was a good basic filter. What else could I use? Remember "Let the trend be your friend"? But how could I put this into practice? Swing lines, or wave patterns, are one tool to define the trend. A strong uptrend is made up of successively higher highs (HH) and higher lows (HL). Conversely, a strong downtrend is made up of successively lower highs (LH) and lower lows (LL). Would it make sense to take only long trades when the overall trend was long? And what about those trends that only fit the trend definition partially—that is, successively higher lows but not necessarily the accompanying higher highs? By keeping track of the swing line trends for each trade on my spreadsheet, this question was easy to answer. Some charting programs will mark the swing line trends for you automatically.

Figure 16.2 illustrates examples of half and full swing line filters; the arrows indicate the direction of the applicable trade. Notice that the filters kept us out of the largest move of the day. On the other hand, they also kept us out of nine small moves

Table 16.3 Trade Sequences, Filtered, August–November 2002

Trade Sequence in Day	No. of Trades Recorded	Profit after Commission ($)	Successful Trades (%)
1	43	62	55
2	40	629	64
3	39	1,076	65

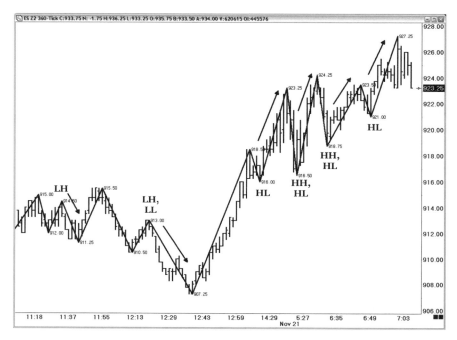

Figure 16.2 Swing Lines as Filters. *Source:* S&P Emini, 360-tick, CME, 11/20–11/21/02.

that would have all been losing trades. The first example is a half filter because there is only one lower high in place. A lower low was subsequently reached. After that, prices broke to a higher high and no trades were available. The next filter is a full filter short because a lower high and a lower low were both in place at the time that the swing began. Note that this chart does not show actual trades; it only shows the filters and applicable directions for trades.

Table 16.4 shows the effect of the three filter types ranged over two time periods during 2002, April to July (strong bear market) and August to November (sideways market). Until late August, I was trading the EN method without any filters other than the time-of-day filter that I have already mentioned. During

Table 16.4 Filtering Trades over Time, 2002

	No. of Trades	Points	Profit after Commission ($)	Successful Trades (%)	Profit per Trade ($)
April 17–August 20					
No filter	715	463.50	16,244	65	22.72
August 20–November 20					
No filter	755	24.95	−6,001	58	−7.95
Half filter	375	119.25	2,363	63	6.30
Full filter	118	90	3,367	71	28.54
August20–November 20, Including the *Enthios Hook* Re-Entry Method					
No filter	1,051	209.50	383	60	0.36
Half filter	589	243.75	6,533	64	11.09
Full filter	231	146.25	5,095	68	22.06

August, I noticed profits slipping away and I scrambled to find a way to filter out bad trades. The trade log spreadsheet saved me. First I introduced the volume filter. In mid-September, I introduced the swing line filter. I also noticed that many trades would fail the first time and then, after a retracement to a specific point—the *Enthios Hook* (see Chapter 17)—would then bounce back up. The inclusion of this new variation further saved the system and brought its profit per trade back to where it was back in the easy days of trading the Bear market.

The results of these various filters are shown in Table 16.4. It is important to note that all of this information was gained from my simple trade log spreadsheet and took only minutes to create the data summaries. Without a trade log, I would be trading as blindly as if I did not have any charts at all.

Note the cataclysmic change in unfiltered EN trades pre- and post-August 20. The method evolved from producing a profit of $16,244 during a four month period, to *losing* $6,001 during a three month period. Did this mean that the method was useless? Possibly. It was clearly a direct reflection of the change in market dynamics from a strong bear market to a sideways market. I had to make some serious changes to the method if it were to survive the new market conditions. Rather than dump the method and look for something else, I chose to pay attention to what was happening and refine the method.

Simply by applying the half swing line filter (on top of the preexisting volume and time of day filters, which again only reflect common sense), I was able to "swing" back into the plus column. Then by applying the full swing line filter, the method became even more profitable overall, yet the number of trades was cut by a third. As a result, profit per trade quadrupled.

Applying the *Enthios Hook* re-entry method further improved results over the same period, particularly for the half filter variation; profits more than doubled from $2,363 to $6,533.

PART FIVE

ENTHIOS REALTIME: PUTTING IT ALL TOGETHER

You have now discovered the basics of Fibonacci, plus several new and original applications of Fibonacci developed by day traders for the intraday market.

By now you should have all of the tools that you need to trade successfully: standard Fibonacci, advanced, and new Fibonacci, an assortment of Enthios.com tools, and guidelines for building good trading habits, including premarket preparation as well as the accumulation of live trading data that you can use to stay ahead of the curve, or at the very least not slip off of it!

This part introduces some of the methods that are available to subscribers of Enthios Realtime. I introduce some fundamentals on which I created a successful, objective trading system. You can take the same fundamentals and build one for yourself.

With knowledge gained from the previous four parts of this book, and with the fundamentals that are introduced in this part, you can build an objective trading system that works for your own needs.

17

THE ENTHIATIC CHART: TRADING FROM THE INSIDE

A WORD ABOUT CONSTANT TICK CHARTS

Several real-time charting software producers offer constant tick charts in addition to time-based charts. The include Ensign Windows, Esignal, TradeStation, and Investor/RT. The difference is that each bar or candle in a time-based chart is made up of a specified number of minutes. Each bar in a 5-minute chart, for example, is exactly five minutes long. This is useful because when you are trading a method that depends on the close of one candle before an order is entered, you already know exactly when that candle will close: In the case of a 5-minute chart, it will close in 5-minute intervals. Each bar in a constant tick chart, however, is made up of a specific number of ticks. Each time a trade is made, that creates one tick. During heavy market trading, there can be over 400 ticks per minute on the S&P Emini. However during a period of light trading, during the overnight trading session, for example, there may be less than 100 ticks per *hour*. Therefore, the bars in a constant tick chart are volume-dependent, not time-dependent. The advantage of a constant tick chart is that you do not have to wait for the time period to expire before entering the trade, particularly if prices and volume are surging. By waiting, you will often miss a portion of the trade. Usually when a price/volume surge occurs, the ticks increase and the bar then closes quickly, immediately starting another bar and, in so doing, triggering the trade. Another advantage of constant tick charts is that you can view the entire day's activity—24-hours—in terms of the number of ticks. In this way, the slow volume levels of the overnight session and the lunchtime session, all appear in context with the high volume of the opening and closing rush. Figure 17.1 illustrates this by showing one 24-hour trading day on a 360-tick chart.

One disadvantage of constant tick charts is that you do not know exactly when one bar will close and the next will begin. Some of the chart software producers include tick counters and other alerts to help monitor the tick count of the current bar.

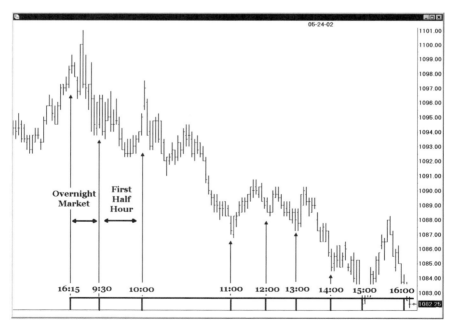

Figure 17.1   Constant Tick Charts. *Source:* S&P Emini, 600-tick, CME, 5/24/02.

TRADE THE RANGE OR THE BREAKOUT?

A fellow named Barry Lutz at Tactrade.com came up with a simple yet elegant solution: trade both the range and the breakout. This appeals to me because I have spent a considerable amount of time trying to determine when to trade the range, and when to trade the breakout. I have read books by the trading masters, some of whom say "don't trade the range, only trade the breakout," but none of them has ever managed to clearly articulate just when to pinpoint a breakout. And, as with most breakouts, if you are not already on the train when it leaves the station, then there is no catching it until it is already half way down the track.

Figure 17.2 shows an example of range trading, from one end of a range to another. The arrows show possible gains.

Figure 17.2 Range Trading. *Source:* S&P Emini, 3-minute, CME, 4/24/02.

Figure 17.3 shows what happens when prices break out of the range or channel.

How to have your cake and it it too? The solution is as shown in Figure 17.4. I call it the Enthiatic Chart, or EN for short.

In Figure 17.4, you see three lines that follow the price bars: a middle line (1) and two outside lines (2) forming the channel. The middle line is a simple moving average of prices. The two outside lines are derivations of the moving average, based upon the average true range of the previous price bars. So if the range of the previous bars was large, then that will push the

Figure 17.3   Breakout Trading. *Source:* S&P Emini, 3-minute, CME, 4/24/02.

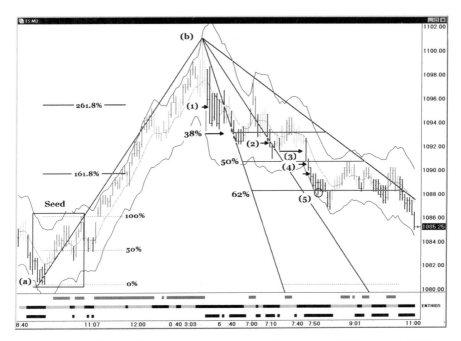

Figure 17.6   Fibonacci Retracement Targets for EN. *Source:* S&P Emini, 360-tick, CME, May 2002.

Trade (1) entered short as shown at 1096, and took two points on the first contract, exiting at the lower band target of 1094. This was also the 38% retracement line. A cautious trader would have taken profits on both contracts here, since the 38% retracement line often provides strong support.

Trade (2) entered as shown, but failed to reach its initial target, which was close to the 50% retracement line. The failure of prices to punch through the 50% retracement line was a strong signal to exit the trade.

The third trade technically entered at point (4), but an aggressive trader would have taken the signal at point (3), where prices dropped below the previous solid down bar, which acted as support. This time, the initial target for the first contract was achieved and a continuation breakout followed. The most logical target was the 62% retracement level of 1088 (5), a 3–4 point gain depending on the entry point.

SUMMARY AND REVIEW

Here is what I hope you have learned from this chapter:

- Trade from the middle to the outside. That way, when you reach the outside, you already have some profits and are well positioned to take advantage of a breakout or continuation move should it then occur.
- Leverage your odds by using multiple shares or contracts and taking profits at realistic points along the way.
- Think about the method that you are using, and how filters can help improve your efficiency.
- Establish an appropriate time frame to trade your method for your selected instrument. Be willing to adapt that to longer or shorter time frames, in response to market conditions.
- You can also combine two methods to maximize profit potential. In the next chapter, I introduce a universal scalping method that works alone but that can also be combined with the EN as an early entry tool.

18

THE RS CHART

The Retracement Scalp (RS) is a simple trading tool that works particularly well during nontrending days. It has three components: an oscillator, a moving average, and a parabolic stop. The premise is straightforward: When the trend changes from short to long, or from long to short, in whatever time period, a retracement or pause normally occurs before the trend resumes. The RS method is designed to take advantage of that. Because the trend can be short-lived, the RS is fine-tuned to capture a very quick profit before the trend can exhaust or reverse itself.

You can use any type of oscillator and any type of moving average. It is best to adjust these to the nature of the instrument you are trading. Figure 18.1 shows a typical RS trade. Once the oscillator indicates a change of direction, you wait for prices to retrace back to the other side of the moving average, then enter the trade one tick beyond that point. In the case of the S&P Emini, the exit target is one point or $50.

The oscillator goes short at point (1). From here, wait for prices to retrace back above the moving average line as they do in the next 1-minute bar. Then enter a limit sell order one tick above the high of the bar that closed above the moving average. This occurred at point (2), at a price of 1089. After entering the trade, immediately set a limit buy order for a one point gain. This occurred at point (3), at 1088. With two contracts, that was a quick gain of $100.

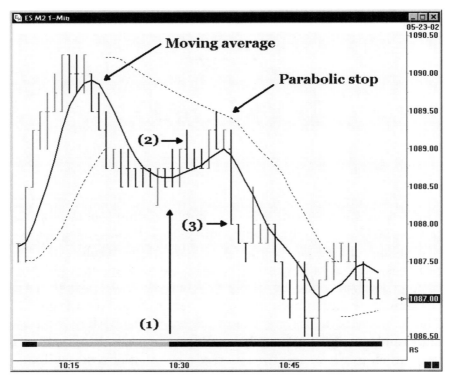

Figure 18.1 RS Chart. *Source:* S&P Emini, 1-minute, CME, 5/23/02.

I find that a parabolic stop is helpful, as shown here. In general I will let the trade move away until a MSH (see Chapter 1) is formed. That MSH will then become the resistance level, and I will set my exit stop one tick above that. If no MSH forms before the Parabolic stop is hit, I will use that as a fail-safe stop.

In trending or breakaway markets, a retracement will not necessarily occur after the oscillator changes direction or, if there is a retracement, it is not sufficient for prices to retrace past the moving average. You can use a shorter moving average, but there is always a balance between missing good trades and filtering out bad trades. It is usually more efficient to find a way to capture more of the upside of the trades that you have entered using an effective filtering system. One way is to use the parabolic stops. This chart shows the advantage of this method; in a breakout situation such as this, the stop stays loose at the beginning and then after 10–15 bars it begins to pull in tight. In this way, it takes advantage of the temporary aspect of price exhaustion: What goes up must come down. However, the drawback to the parabolic stop is that it only really works after those first 10–15 bars. And a price trend will often reverse then turn again in less than 10 bars, a situation far too volatile for the parabolic stops to work.

You can also stay in the trade longer by integrating the shorter time frame RS chart into the EN chart.

COMBINING THE RS AND EN CHARTS

One aspect of the EN chart that can be applied directly to the RS chart is that of trading two contracts, taking one profit at a fixed first profit target and holding the second contract for the potential continuation.

How do you know where to fix the first profit target? Simply refer to the trade records that you have been keeping in your trade log, where you marked the maximum potential for each trade. Now click on the RS filter so that you only see RS trades. By taking an average of the most efficient exit points of the past 200 trades, you can have a continually up to date optimized exit target. The same applies to stops, by filtering the "wiggle" or lowest point of each trade.

Once you have optimized the exit target for your first contract, you are left with the question of how to exit the second contract. You may use Fibonacci again; even better, I have observed that often—though not always—a trade on the shorter time frame RS chart (1-minute) leads into a trade on the EN chart (360-tick). That is, I will be short first on the RS chart,

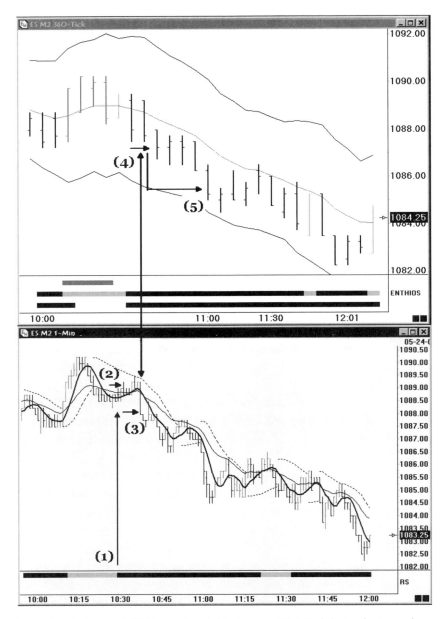

Figure 18.2 RS and EN Charts Overlaid. *Source:* S&P Emini, 1-minute and 360-tick, CME, 5/24/02.

then when I am about to cover that short position, I notice that the EN chart is about to go short. Why not just hold those two contracts from the RS trade, with one point of profit in hand for each contract, and switch over to the EN chart to manage the rest of the trade?

Figure 18.2 shows the same trade as Figure 18.1, this time overlaid with the EN chart. As with Figure 18.1, the RS chart in Figure 18.2 shows (1) the oscillator switching short, (2) the subsequent retracement to the moving average and short entry at 1089, and (3) the 1-point target achieved at 1088. Now follow

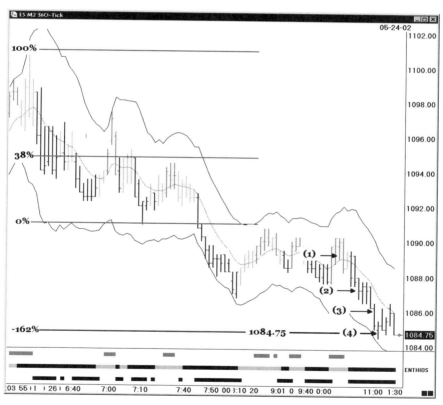

Figure 18.3   Fibonacci on the Combined RS-EN Chart. *Source:* S&P Emini, 1-minute and 360-tick, CME, 5/24/02.

the line up from (3) to the respective bar in the 360-tick EN chart. The RS is already short at this point, with 1 point ($50 per contract) in hand. The same bar in the EN chart (4) has signaled a short entry, and is waiting for a trigger, which comes in the subsequent bar. The short entry for the EN trade would have been at 1087.25, but we are already short at 1089. The target for the first contract of the EN trade is 1086, shown at point (5). This is a profit of 3 points per contract, compared to 1 point for the RS trade and 1.25 points for the EN trade. We can now use Fibonacci to target the second contract for a potential continuation; Figure 18.3 shows that the calculated –162% target for W3 is 1084.75.

Taking this another step, Figure 18.3 shows the use of Fibonacci with the EN trade that began as a RS trade.

The original RS entry was at (1), the EN entry would have been at (2), the first contract covered at (3), and the second contract covered at (4), the W3 target.

SUMMARY AND REVIEW

- The Retracement Scalp (RS) works well in nontrending markets, and as an early entry for trending trades.
- Shorter term charts can be used to gain better entry for longer term trades, with relatively low risk.
- Fibonacci targets can be used for continuation trade exits across any time frame.

19

THE HANDY CHART: COMBINING TIME FRAMES AND INDICATORS

Most of the trading methods in this book are based on patterns and on calculating targets once certain patterns are in place.

Typically, traders divide themselves into two types: the pattern traders and the technical analysis traders. They tend to be mutually exclusive, that is, pattern traders shun the bevy of lines, signals and curling, crossing, widening and narrowing channels that complicate charts. They feel that technical indicators make you weak because they keep you from seeing what you should be able to see simply by looking at a chart. Technical traders sometimes overdo it with "holy grail" type setups that look mighty impressive and complicated, but often tend to mask what really is happening underneath. However, technical analysis can be very useful as long as you are aware of what the indicators are telling you, and as long as you are aware that most indicators just tell you what you *should* be able to see with the naked eye, anyhow.

I like to use a combination of both. The EN method is clearly a pattern-based method, with some technical indicators (let's call them road signs) used to set the entry triggers and stops.

The Handy Chart, on the other hand, is pure technical analysis. It is a method that uses a deliberate combination of technical indicators and no patterns at all, other than the pattern of indicators that I chose, specifically because those indicators complement each other and work as a team. Together the pattern-based EN method works with the technical based Handy Chart described here, to form a two-method system.

THE STOCHASTIC

Combining different time frames in the same chart makes good use of the greater trend (from a longer time frame) as a filter from which to trade the same signals but on a shorter time frame. One way is to use the crossing of fast and slow moving averages, as in the Chimpanzee Cross (see Chapter 11). Another is to use a fast and slow stochastic. The faster stochastic represents a shorter time period, and the slower stochastic represents a longer time period. The stochastic oscillator is a momentum indicator that shows the location of the current close relative to the high/low range averaged over a set number of periods. Standard use of the stochastic has a high band of about 80% and a low band of about 20%. When the stochastic is above the 80% band, prices are overbought. When the stochastic then drops below the 80% band, that serves as a sell signal.

Although most traders use the stochastic to presage directional change, I used it in the Handy Chart to show shifts of momentum. The ergodic indicator does a better job of showing directional change. Therefore, instead of looking at a cross above or below the 80/20 bands on the stochastic, I am only interested in the difference between the fast and slow stochastic lines. Accordingly, I create a histogram that shows the positive or negative difference between the two.

A momentum indicator on its own will not be reliable enough, even if it takes into consideration multiple time frames.

I have also identified three other useful indicators. These are discussed next.

THE ERGODIC

The ergodic is similar to the stochastic, but rather than indicating momentum, it is effective for pinpointing turning points. The ergodic indicator is an average of an average of the net change, divided by an average of an average of the absolute value of the net change. It points out likely turning points which can then be authenticated using the stochastic and Bollinger indicators.

THE BOLLINGER BANDS

As we saw in Chapter 12, Bollinger Bands take a standard moving average of prices, and apply a standard deviation of those prices to determine the volatility of the price movement over the selected time period. When prices surge in either direction, the bands will widen. When prices narrow into a tight trading range, the bands also narrow. I have created an indicator that measures the relative width of the Bollinger Bands, and the direction of change (wider or narrower). Once the bands have narrowed to a certain point, the likelihood of a sudden breakout increases. The direction of that breakout has usually already been foretold by the ergodic, and confirmed by the stochastic.

THE PARABOLIC

Originally developed by Welles Wilder (creator of the RSI and ATR), the parabolic SAR is more popular for setting stops than for establishing direction or trend. That is also how I use it. A quick glance at Figure 19.1 shows how the parabolic stop works—

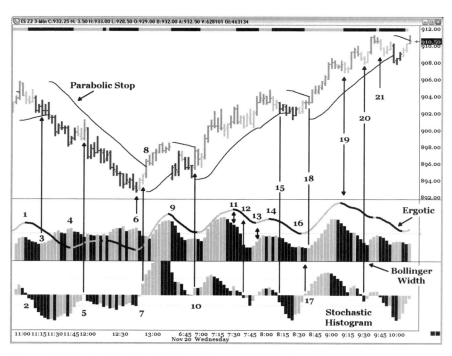

Figure 19.1   Enthios Handy Chart. *Source:* S&P Emini, 3-minute, CME, 11/19–11/20/02.

it starts off quite far from the entry price. As time and prices move away from the trade entry, the stop tightens proportionate to time and price movement, as the likelihood of a price reversal increases.

THE METHOD

For trade entry, I am looking for at least two of the four indicators to be in agreement. If I am feeling more conservative, I will wait for three of the four to be in agreement. Refer to Figure 19.1 to demonstrate how it works:

1. The ergodic signals a potential direction change. Now we look for confirmations from the other indicators.

2. The fast stochastic crosses the slow downward, indicating a change of acceleration rate. Prices could still be oversold; we are not interested in the oversold or overbought condition, only in the change of acceleration rate between the two time frames, fast and slow. At this point, prices are still above the parabolic stop; the Bollinger Bands are decreasing in width. So conditions are not yet ripe for a conservative short.

3. At the point several bars later, the Bollinger Bands have reached their narrowest point and are beginning to widen. The change in color of the Bollinger bars signifies that the bands are widening. The first time this occurs after a period of narrowing, is often the signal of an emerging breakout. Note also that prices are touching the parabolic stop. Now all four of our indicators line up. As soon as prices drop, we will want to enter the short. That occurs two bars later.

4. Here is our first sign of a potential directional change, the ergodic. This illustrates one of the problems with using a combination of indicators: It never takes long to get a reversal or exit signal, and the trader with jumpy fingers will usually exit the trade at the first such signal. When you have all four indicators lined up to enter a trade, it is often best to wait for at least two of those same indicators to tell you to get out of the trade and, sometimes, even three. This is where subjectivity comes in. At this point, we have a tidy profit and are quite far from the parabolic stop. The stochastic is decelerating, but is still showing short; Bollinger Bands are neutral at this point.

5. Here the stochastic has crossed long. Bollinger Bands are tightening. Three of the four indicators are telling us to exit. We will exit as soon as prices move above the high of

the current bar. As it turns out, that bar was the high point. Prices fall back down. The ergodic is still signaling a reversal short, but that is conflicting with the stochastic, which is short once again. Note the time of day. Prices are drifting lower. The ergodic goes back into agreement with the stochastic, and our confidence level increases.

6. Finally, at this point, the ergodic again signals a potential directional change.

7. Two bars later, the stochastic moves forcefully into agreement.

8. One bar later, prices finally break the parabolic stop, which is a stop: No matter what else the signals are telling us, if prices cross the stop we exit the trade. Note the time: 3:55 P.M. The equities market is about to close, and with these indicators all calling for long, we are not surprised when we see short covering going into the close of the futures.

9. Next morning, the ergodic signals a short reversal. The Bollinger Bands are too wide though, and stochastic are still long, so we reject the trade, even though prices are below the parabolic.

10. At 10:00, the market shows its hand, putting in a higher low and a 123 long reversal. The ergodic goes long, stochastic histogram bounces back long, and the Bollinger Bands are widening. We can enter now or wait until prices break the parabolic.

11. Ergodic is suggesting reversal and the Bollinger Bands are tightening. However the stochastic histogram is still crossed up, showing that the shorter time frame stochastic is still under-bought compared to the longer time frame. We will stay in the trade.

12. At this point, the Bollinger Bands are quite narrow and the stochastic histogram has crossed short. We will exit on the trailing stop.

13. Four periods later, the stop has not yet been hit; both the ergodic and the stochastic have bounced back long and the Bollinger Bands are widening. We're still long.

14. The ergodic signals short.

15. The stochastic signals short and prices touch the parabolic stop. We will exit below this price.

16. The ergodic signals a long.

17. In the next bar, the stochastic signals a momentum shift long.

18. The Bollinger Bands reverse from narrowing to widening, and the parabolic stop is touched. We will go long above the high of this bar.

19. The ergodic signals short and the Bollinger Bands are declining, however the Stochastic is still long. With only two indicators in agreement, we stay long until either three indicators agree, or the parabolic stop is hit, whichever comes first.

20. All three indicators—ergodic, Bollinger, and stochastic—are in agreement. We would exit below the low of this bar, but prices moved up from here.

21. We finally exit the trade here, as prices move back down and the other three indicators are in agreement.

20

FULL CIRCLE: COMBINING METHODS TO CREATE A SYSTEM

Excuse me if I appear to go back to Chapter 1 to continue the discussion on the Building Blocks of price action; perhaps I should have just appended this last chapter to the first. Indeed I feel so strongly about the importance of those basic building blocks of price action that I have included in the Appendix an excellent article on that subject written by a trading friend, Judy MacKeigan, whom most of us know as "Buffy." Before you get to that, however, allow me to tie up a few loose ands and hopefully, in so doing, reach a methodical conclusion to this book.

If the market had only one type of signature, it would be easy to create a method of trading that was curve-fit for that signature. We could all automate it and then go off and do other things while our computers made money for us. Of course, if that were possible, then everybody would be doing it. The market appears to naturally compensate against any rhyme or reason by maintaining an unbiased chaos that will render any static method obsolete by the time that method becomes productive. This is the nature of the auction marketplace. So the superstitious traders protect their methods, believing that if nobody else learns about them, they will be alone in trading it. They are wrong.

The reality is, whenever a particular method seems to work over a particular period of time, the market seems to change its course, its pace, its direction, its breath, if only long enough to completely contradict the theory behind that system. Is it a conscious decision made by "the market"? Of course not. It simply demonstrates that the market is dynamic. All we have to do is understand its ever-changing nature. If we can break the market down into its fundamentals, into the smallest common denominators of price-action models, and if we can then develop methods that work for each price-action model independent from each other, then we have the workings of a system: a grouping of methods that work well together. Add to that the ability to adjust the individual methods using the filters and trading habits that we already discussed, and we have a system that is both objective and adaptable. And with that, we can trade with confidence in any market. We still have to be in front of the computer pushing the buttons. Or do we?

ARE YOU NOSTRADAMUS?

If you are Nostradamus, you don't need to read any further. But if you are unable to predict the future, then what follows may be of some interest.

My trading turned around the moment I admitted that I had no idea, whatsoever, *what* was going to happen in the market, even from one moment to the next. All around me, in trading chat rooms that I frequent, in the e-mail lists and newsletters that I subscribe to, people boast that they know what is going to happen. "We're going up from here." "This is a bottom. Well, if not, it's close anyhow." But if you try to pin them down and ask what their specific trade entry and exit would be, they always seem to back away from the specific claim with the trump phrase "Oh, well you have to make that decision for yourself."

The problem is that, because no one really knows what is going to happen next, anyone can be right 50% of the time. Actually, they're right more often than that because the way markets trade, with price action up and down and back and forth all day, one person can go long at one price, and another person can go short at the same price at the same time, and both can end up with a profit. Unfortunately, what happens far more often is that those two people both end up losing money on their respective trades due to the usual overdose of either fear, or greed, or both.

TWO TYPES OF PRICE ACTION: TRADING RANGES AND BREAKOUTS

I still have not found a way to predict what will happen in the market, at least to the extent that I can make clear trading decisions based on any kind of meaningful predictions. But along the way I realized that it really does not matter. Indeed, the more you wed yourself to a particular outcome, the more you set yourself up both for failure and for inflexibility when things change. I realized that rather than trying to predict things, it would be far more productive to try to understand the basic building blocks of market movement, and to then construct an idiot-proof trading system based on those basics. Trading success requires being right more often than being wrong; but it would not be realistic to expect to be right all of the time.

One of the most important observations is the nature of price action. All of the price action in the market can be broken into two types: trading ranges and breakouts. There is no way to know how long prices will stay in a range, and there is no way to know how long they will continue in a breakout. The solution was to develop a system made up of three trading models: one that works well in a trading range, one that gets you out of the range and at least part way into a breakout, and one that can ride the bigger wave of a major continuation move from that breakout. Let's look first at some of the aspects of these two types of price action.

Horizontal Trading Ranges

There are many types of trading ranges, but to me these can be subdivided into two major types: the kind that move sideways and the kind that move diagonally. The sideways trading range is characterized by congestion, consolidation, and ledges. Figure 20.1 shows a horizontal trading range.

Normally a horizontal trading range can be identified because a moving average changes from having a diagonal slope to

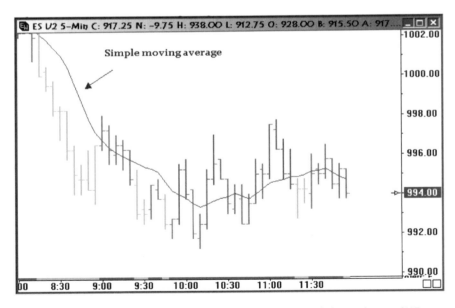

Figure 20.1   Horizontal Trading Range. *Source:* S&P Emini, 5-minute, CME, 11/26/02.

a horizontal slope. Some horizontal trading ranges can be traded profitably; others cannot. This one cannot.

The next horizontal trading range in Figure 20.2 *can* be traded profitably because prices move both above and below the moving average for more than two consecutive price bars. In all of these charts, bars indicate buying and selling opportunities. The gray bars represent dead price bars that are hanging too close to the moving average. The trend lines are created using a 2-standard deviation Regression Channel.

Figure 20.2 Tradable Horizontal Trading Range. *Source:* S&P Emini, 360-tick, CME, 11/26/02.

Diagonal Trading Ranges

The second type of trading range is diagonal. Some might call this a trend; however, it is still a type of trading range in that it has definable upper and lower points within a channel. Prices trend in a specific direction, but the oscillation above and below the moving average allows both short and long trades while riding the general trend up, as shown in Figure 20.3.

With the advantage of hindsight, we can see with great clarity the trading range represented by the regression channel. However at the time each bar is forming, you have no clue

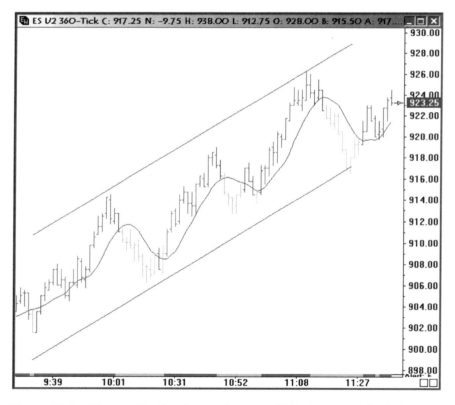

Figure 20.3   Diagonal Trading Range. *Source:* S&P Emini, 360-tick, CME, 11/26/02.

whether the longer term trend will continue or not. Now let's look at the other type of price action.

Breakouts

The second type of price action is the *breakout*. This is character-ized by prices leaving the moving average and seldom, if at all, touching that moving average. Figure 20.4 shows a breakout.

Figure 20.4   Breakout. *Source:* S&P Emini, 360-tick, CME, 11/26/02.

Breakouts usually end in either a consolidation pattern (horizontal trading range) or reversal back up (another breakout). In the case of a reversal back up, quite often the slope of the reversal is equal to that of the original breakout, forming a "V" pattern.

The problem, of course, is that the two possible outcomes provide no indication as to when, or how to trade into and out of a breakout or trading range. Figure 20.5 illustrates the problem.

Figure 20.5 Breakout from Horizontal Range. *Source:* S&P Emini, 360-tick, CME, 11/26/02.

Breakouts rarely occur on the first attempt out of a trading range. They also often occur in the opposite direction than the first indication would imply. In Figure 20.5 you can see two attempts to break down out of the horizontal range. You can also see several attempts to break up out of the top of the range. Then prices dropped. Horizontal ranges tend to act as ledges in the greater trend, and you may locate the breakout from the trading range in the same direction from which it came. So if prices were trending down, you would expect the eventual breakout (continuation) to be down. But this is very often not the case. Figure 20.6 shows an example of a breakout down from a trading range in the opposite direction from which it entered. Note that this chart includes the previous examples from Figures 20.2, 20.3, and 20.5.

WHERE TO NOW?

The direction of breakout cannot be predicted with any certainty. The direction and timing are both equally elusive. Now armed with the knowledge that only the past can be predicted, and also armed with a basic understanding of the two different types of price movement, the next step is to develop a system made up of those three trading models that I mentioned earlier: one that works well in a trading range, one that gets you out of the range and at least part way into a breakout, and one that can ride the big wave of a major continuation move from that breakout.

A key component of the system is making sure that the three methods do not conflict with one other. Therefore, the single most important rule is this: Each method, individually, should be profitable across all types of price movement, at least in the longer term. The implication is that each method should be able to perform on its own without either of the others. Then by stacking them up on top of each other, the sum of

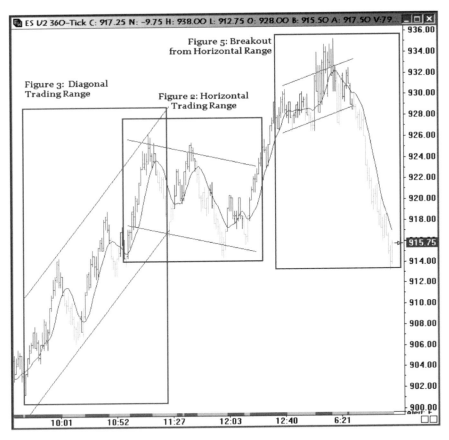

Figure 20.6   Price Action Types.

the methods becomes greater than the whole. The confirmation that each provides to the others is where you gain your real advantage.

To summarize, we are looking for these three methods:

1. Range Method +
2. Breakout Method +
3. Continuation Method =

Range Method

You may choose from many range trading methods. Some involve Bollinger bands; others involve dynamic regression channels, such as the method that I wrote about in Chapter 6. I have adjusted that method to fit into this system and now call it the EN Chart, which I introduced in Chapter 17. Another good range method is the RS, which can be combined with the EN.

Breakout Method

The EN method also captures breakouts from the range. As explained in Chapter 17, the first contract is traded from the middle of a range to the outside, with the likelihood that prices will then reverse back into the range. If this happens you scratch on the second contract, nothing lost. But if prices surge beyond the edge of the trading range, then you still have the second contract and can now take advantage of the fact that during a breakout, prices tend to move *relatively* directly toward the next obvious price point, such as an overnight high or low, or a major point of support or resistance, or perhaps a Fibonacci target. The problem occurs when there is more than one target. To be conservative, you should take your profits on the second contract at the next major price target along the way because that is precisely where the upward surge will pivot and possibly fail. But so often, after that target has been reached and you have taken profits on your second contract, prices then continue back up and, if you are not in the trade, they will go beyond.

Once you have taken your modest profit on the Range Method, and once you have then taken a profit on the first major push of a breakout, how do you capture the bigger move?

Continuation Method

One answer is to simply trade more contracts, and use the Japanese method of selling half at the first clear exit point, half again at the next, and so on. The problem with this is that if you start with 8 contracts, in expectation of dropping them off along the way of the big breakout, these breakouts do not occur very often. You may end up dropping most of these contracts as stops or as scratches (break-even), and the only one who profits from that is the broker.

Another method is to aim for no target at all; rather, simply run with the prices, yet capture profits as close to the peak as possible. Such a method should minimize losses during the horizontal trading periods where your range trading method is producing swing profits. That is exactly what the Handy Chart shown in Figure 20.7 does.

THE SYSTEM

Now you can combine the three methods, and trade them continuously, to form a system. For example, I trade two contracts using the Enthiatic Chart to generate profits for the Range and Breakout Method, and trade another two contracts using the Handy Chart as my Continuation Method. They don't always overlap, and during periods of whipsaws drawdowns do occur, but Figures 20.7 and 20.8 show examples of how the three methods can be structured to work together. Both charts cover the same time period, the afternoon of November 21, 2002. Times are in Pacific Standard Time.

Figure 20.7 is the Handy Chart that was described in Chapter 19. During the afternoon period there were four trades, as shown. The dotted lines indicate the net gain or loss of the trade from start to finish. The first one, a short, exited flat (even). The second one, a long, exited at a small loss. The third one, a short, exited again at a small loss. The fourth one was able to capture a reasonable gain on the end of day trade. Note, in hindsight, the sideways movement of the market. Note how the Handy Chart was able to minimize losses until a real breakout occurred.

LIST OF FIGURES
AND TABLES

————

Appendix

PRICE ACTION—
THE FOOTPRINT OF MONEY

by Judy MacKeigan (Buffy)

"What is price action?" is a frequently asked question by aspiring traders. Traders who ask, feel it is a well-kept secret when all they receive for an answer is: 'Swing highs, swing lows, test of top/bottom, and so on, are all price action.' The answer still leaves them in the dark. Understanding price action enables a trader to minimize questionable entries and improve exits. Price action is the footprint of the money.

Let's start with the very basics. The bars on the chart on the next page are labeled as traders commonly referred to them:

- *Up Bar:* is a bar with a higher high and higher low than the previous bar. The bars marked off are in an up trend. Notice how the close is higher than the open until what turns out to be the last bar of the trend where the close is

This article originally appeared on www.dacharts.com and on the www
.ensignsoftware.com website.

lower than the open. There were more sellers then buyers on the last bar.

- *Down Bar:* is a bar with a lower high and lower low than the previous bar. The bars marked off are in a down trend. Notice how the close is lower than the open until what turns out to be the last bar of the trend where the close is higher than the open. There were more buyers then sellers on the last bar.

- *Inside Bar:* also called a *narrow range bar,* is a bar with the high that is lower than the previous bar and low that

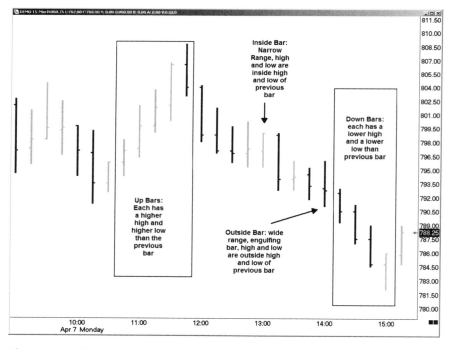

Figure A.1 Up, Down, Inside, Outside. *Source:* S&P Emini, 15-minute, CME, 10/08/2002.

is higher than the previous bar. Some traders do not consider an inside bar that has either an equal high or an equal low as an inside bar, others do. Inside bars usually represent market indecision. As on any bar, the closer the open and close are to each other shows just how undecided the market is as neither the buyers or sellers are in control. Buyers are in control on the inside bar marked on the chart because the close is at the top of the bar.

- *Outside Bar:* also called a Wide Range or Engulfing Bar, is a bar with a high that is higher than the previous bar and with a low that is lower than the previous bar thereby engulfing the previous bar. Since the open and close are close together on the marked bar, neither the buyers or the sellers are in control and the market is undecided which way to go.

When the open is in the bottom quarter/third of the bar and the close is in the top quarter/third of the bar, it is said to be bullish engulfing with the buyers in control. When the open is in the top quarter/third of the bar and the close is in the bottom quarter/third, it is said to be bearish engulfing with the sellers in control.

Another definition used for this bar—especially if candlestick charts are used—is that the open and close have to engulf the previous bars open and close and not just the high and low of the bar. With this definition, the wide range bar or engulfing bar does not need to have a higher high or lower low to qualify. The first definition most probably came about with bar charts where it is harder to notice the open and close.

The following chart has the swing highs and lows marked in both an up trend and a down trend. Price on a given time frame is in an up trend if it is making a higher highs (HH) and a high lows (HL) and in a down trend if it is making lower highs (LH) and lower lows (LL). If price is doing anything else,

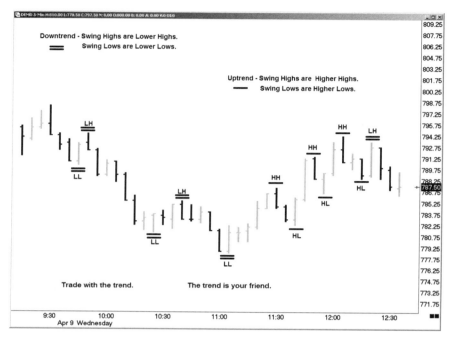

Figure A.2   Trade with the Trend. *Source:* S&P Emini, 5-minute, CME, 10/08/02.

it is in a consolidation pattern—range, triangle, pennant, rectangle, and so on.

The trend is considered in place until price is no longer making higher highs and higher lows in an up trend or lower highs and lower lows in a down trend. After a trend is broken, there is usually a period of consolidation that is easier to see on a lower time frame. With practice, you will be able to visualize this going on without looking at the lower time frame.

When price is in a consolidation pattern that is often referred to as chop, it is usually in a range with no trend pattern to the swing highs and lows.

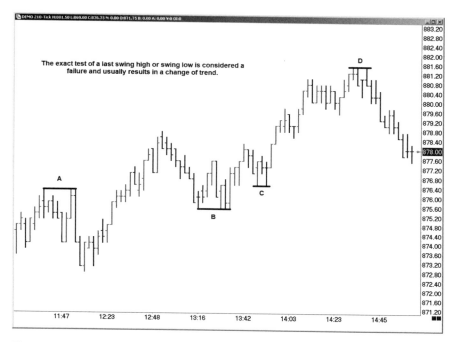

Figure A.3 Exact Tests (Double Tops and Bottoms). *Source:* S&P Emini, 210-tick, 12/30/02.

The Figure A.3 shows how an exact test of high or low may mean a change in trend as it failed to make a higher high on test of last swing high or a lower low on test of last swing low:

a. Price was making HHs and HLs until price tested the prior swing high at A.

b. Price made a LL and LH until price tested the prior swing low at B.

c. Price made a LH (The bar that does not touch line at C) until price tested the prior swing low at C.

d. Price was making HHs and HLs until price tested the prior swing high at D.

It is possible for one time frame to be in one trend and another time frame to be in a different trend or show consolidation. This is where the phrase "trend within a trend" regarding price action and the different time frames comes from. An example would be that while price may be rising on a daily chart, the intra-day chart will show retracements, corrections of various types and consolidation periods.

The true meaning of this and how it can influence your trading, eludes many. The following exercise is an excellent way to learn what the phrase "trend within trend" means visually.

Pull up a 15-minute chart and mark the highs as higher high (HH) or lower high (LH) and the lows as lower low (LL) or higher low (HL), as shown in Figure A.4. You can also print out

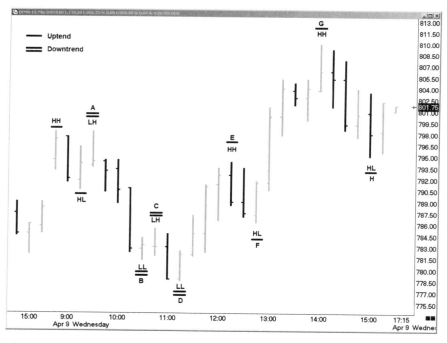

Figure A.4   15-Minute Trend. *Source:* S&P Emini, 15-minute, CME, 10/08/02.

the chart and mark it by hand. Use double lines if price in a down trend and a single line if price in an up trend. Remember price is in an up trend if it is making HH—and HL and in a down trend if it is making LH and LL. If price is doing anything else, it can be a consolidation pattern—range, triangle, pennant, rectangle, and so on.

Points labeled A through D on the example chart are in a down trend. Points labeled E through H are in an up trend.

Now take the same chart and change the time frame to a 5 minutes chart, keeping the letters and lines from the 15 minute by using the padlock with the L to lock lines in Ensign. Mark the new highs and lows that now show with lower case letters and double dash lines for down trend or numbers and single dash lines for an up trend. The result is shown in Figure A.5:

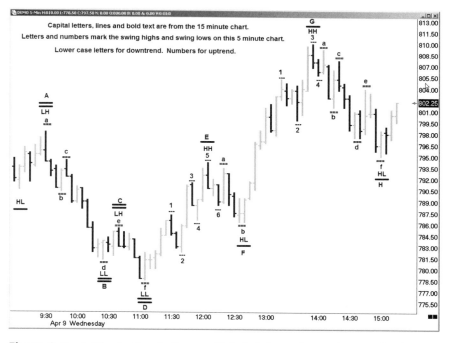

Figure A.5 5-Minute Trend. *Source:* S&P Emini, 5-minute, CME, 10/08/02.

Now we can see by the single or double bold lines below the capital letters what the trend in on the 15 minute at the same time we are able to see the trend on the 5 minute.

Both charts are in a down trend until the 5 minute makes a HH at the first #1. The down trend is broken on the 5M when the LH at e is exceeded. Price then goes on to make a HL starting an up trend that continues until price makes a lower high at the a. The 15 minute just made a HH at the E and will not make a HL until F. At this point, we are expecting a HL on the 15 minute, and are waiting for a long signal on the 5 minute. Some traders would take the entry on the pair of reversal bars at b, others would wait until the last swing high at a is exceeded.

The time frames are now in agreement (shown by #1–#4) up to the HH at G. After the HH at G, the 5 minute goes into a down trend (shown by a-f) to what is still a HL on the 15 minute at H. So, while the 15 minute price action shows only two trends, the 5 minute shows five different trends!

While you may trade the trends on the smaller time frame, waiting for price action to show it is going to move in the same direction as the larger time frame is trading with the trend. The trend is your friend!

GLOSSARY

Citizen's Trading Range (CTR) The first move up, and down, at the beginning of each day. This is usually measured on a 1-minute chart and the Fibonacci target ratios of 1.62 and 2.62 are applied. See Figure 9.1.

Continuation retracement A continuation retracement is a correction wave that retraces to less than 50% of the previous range, then continues back up. Typically, though not always, this is representative of a continuation move in the direction of the prior trend. Refer to Table 2.2.

Correction waves Waves that move counter to the overall trend, providing a natural retracement for the next wave in the direction of the trend. In an uptrend 5-wave sequence, waves 2 and 4 are corrections waves. Refer to Figure 2.7.

Divergence When the oscillation of price action diverges from the oscillation of underlying indicators (MACD, stochastics, etc.), this is the first sign of a weakening of trend, which in turn can lead to sideways congestion or a reversal of trend. Refer to Figure 6.4.

Double bottom Two price bars or candles, not necessarily consecutive, that both have the same low and which occur at the bottom (or potential bottom) of a downtrend. The double bottom is one pattern indicator that most chartists recognize as a strong indicator signaling or predicting a change in price direction. Ideally the first bar of the double bottom will be a down bar, and the second will be an up bar. A double bottom is also one type of MSL. See Figure 1.2.

Double top   Two price bars or candles, not necessarily consecutive, that both have the same high and which occur at the top (or potential top) of a uptrend. The double top is one pattern indicator that most chartists recognize as a strong indicator signaling or predicting a change in price direction. Ideally the first bar of the double top will be an up bar, and the second will be a down bar. A double top is also one type of MSH.

Lower Value Area (LVA)   The lower extent of the Value Area in the Price Histogram. See Figure 10.1.

Market Structure High (MSH)   The opposite of a MSL is a Market Structure High (MSH). It is the first sign of a potential reversal in prices from an uptrend to a downtrend. A MSH is usually made up of three consecutive candles: A high, a higher high, and then a lower high. See Figure 1.3.

Market Structure Low (MSL)   A Market Structure Low (MSL) is the first sign of a potential reversal in prices from a downtrend to an uptrend. It is usually made up of three consecutive candles: A low, a lower low, and then a higher low. See Figure 1.1.

Mechanical stop   A mechanical stop is an order that is placed with your broker to sell your long position if prices move back down to a specific number. Typically a mechanical stop is placed as a market stop order.

Mental stop   A mental stop, as the name suggests, is one that is placed only in your mind. It allows you the flexibility to consider other information as the trade progresses.

MSH-failure entry   The third of three methods to enter a wave. Least risky, but with lowest reward and highest degree of exposure. Go long at the break (failure) of the previous MSH. This is also the registration point of the wave pattern. Refer to Figure 3.2.

MSL-trigger entry   The second of three methods to enter a wave trade. Less risky than a pullback trigger, the reward is also correspondingly lower and the stop correspondingly higher. Trade is triggered when prices move one tick above the high of the third candle of the MSL. Refer to Figure 3.2.

Point of Control (POC)   In the Price Histogram, the price or prices where traders spent the "most amount of time" during the day. See Figure 10.1.

Price Histogram   A chart that shows the relative amount of time spent at each price point during the day. See Figure 10.1.

Pullback entry   The first—and earliest—of three methods to enter a wave trade. As prices pull back form the previous MSH, enter one tick above the high of the previous pullback candle, up to the fourth new low in a price retracement from the previous MSH. Refer to Figure 3.2.

Retracement pivots   Fibonacci ratios drawn from the start (low) of a trend to the finish (high) of that trend, used to gauge the subsequent retracement back down in the opposite direction. Typical important pivots are 0.38 (38%), 0.50 (50%), and 0.62 (62%). For example, if a long trend starts at 100 and rises to 120, 110 represents a 50% retracement back down.

Reversal candle   A reversal candle is the first "down" candle after a series of "up" candles, that is, a candle that closes below its open. In a series of down candles, it is the first up candle in the series, that is, a candle that closes above its open. Refer to Figure 3.5.

Reversal retracement A reversal retracement is a correction wave that retraces more than 50% of the previous range. Typically, though not always, this is representative of the beginning of a reversal in direction of the prior trend. Refer to Table 2.2.

Support/Resistance (S/R) When support is broken, in a downtrend, it always becomes resistance for any move back up. When resistance is broken, in an uptrend, it always become support for any move back down.

Seed retracement The first retracement back down from a potential seed wave. The seed wave is always W1 in a sequence, and the seed retracement is always W2. Targets can be combined from both the seed wave and the seed retracement, to fine-tune a target zone for the top of W3. See Figures 4.2 and 4.3.

Seed Wave The first wave in a sequence of waves, from which the subsequent waves grow. A seed wave always occurs at the point of reversal. For example, after a downtrend, the first wave back up in the opposite direction is a seed wave. It is only confirmed to be a seed wave after a 123 reversal has been identified and registered.

Upper Value Area (UVA) The upper extent of the Value Area in the Price Histogram. See Figure 10.1.

Value Area (VA) The area of prices in the Price Histogram where prices spent 70% of the day. Prices outside of this area are considered to be statistically insignificant. See Figure 10.1.

Wave pattern The combination of an advance, a retracement, and another *higher* advance forms a wave pattern. Note how the wave pattern is made up of a MSL, followed by a MSH, followed by a higher MSL. Refer to Figure 2.3.

RESOURCE GUIDE

RECOMMENDED READING

Candlesticks, Fibonacci, and Chart Pattern Trading Tools
By Robert Fischer and Jens Fischer

By merging 3 of the most popular technical tools used by stock, options, and futures traders, Fibonacci expert Robert Fischer provides a cutting-edge new trading strategy. This synergistic approach—never before written about—will attract traders looking for an edge in challenging market times, regardless of whether they are short- or long-term traders.

$89.95   **Item #T191X-1199025**

Fibonacci Applications and Strategies for Traders
By Robert Fischer

A fresh look at classic principles and applications of Fibonacci numbers and the Elliott Wave trading system. Demonstrates how to calculate and predict key turning points in commodity markets, analyze business and economic cycles as well as identify profitable turning points in interest rate movement. Forty charts and tables show how to use this analysis on a daily, weekly or Intraday trading basis.

$60.00   **Item #T191X-2470**

Secrets of the Undergroundtrader
By Russell Lockhart and Jea Yu

Thoroughly details the most advanced and successful methods of trading used today—stochastics, candlesticks, 3-price breaks, volatility signals, and more. Yu and Lockhart provide step-by-step instructions to easily guide the reader through each method so they can learn it, get comfortable with it, and implement it in any market. A "must-have" for any active, aggressive trader or investor.

$39.95   **Item #T191X-1629004**

The Candlestick Course
By Steve Nison

Get instruction from the expert in Candlestick Charting, Steve Nison. In this easy-to-understand book, Nison explains the practical applications of this hot new trend. By providing quizzes, Q&As, and intensive examples, Nison gives readers the knowledge they need to get involved in this new financial concept.

$59.95   **Item #T191X-84668**

WEBSITES OF INTEREST

www.undergroundtrader.com

Underground trader is a premium real time trading chatroom and training site that specializes in trading U.S. equities, e-minis futures, as well as bonds and currencies.

www.kingcambo.com

KingCAMBO operates a "Chat Room," that provides its members with opinions and commentaries on securities and trading markets and trading market indicators. They also provide their members with public information regarding securities and analyses of securities market indicators and offers them a vehicle to exchange ideas with one another.

www.dacharts.com

daCharts is a community of traders helping traders. Their main focus is the e-Mini S&P500 and Nasdaq100 futures. Participants post their charts to compare insights during the trading day and after-hours. On a typical weekday over 200 charts are posted.

www.ensignsoftware.com

Ensign Software develops charting software for Stock and Commodity traders. Our products use data feeds from eSignal, BMI, and Data Transmission Network (DTN).

www.tradingeducators.com

Trading Educators, Inc. (formerly Ross Trading International, Inc.) was founded in 1988, and has thousands of satisfied customers who have used the Joe Ross methods to produce significant positive results in the markets. Trading Educators, Inc. is registered with the Commodity Futures Trading Commission (CFTC), and the National Futures Association (NFA). Their Mission is to teach you everything you need to know to achieve your financial goals through trading futures.

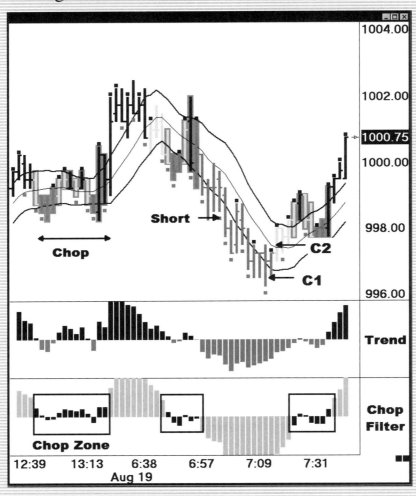

Enthios.com
Making sense out of chaos

1004.00

1002.00

1000.75

1000.00

Short →

← C2

998.00

Chop

← C1

996.00

Trend

Chop Zone

Chop Filter

12:39   13:13   6:38   6:57   7:09   7:31

Aug 19

Enthios.com is a "virtual closet" filled with over 100 web pages of information on trading, and features a discussion group with over 1,000 active members. We also offer premium services:

Carta Diem

Seize the chart! A daily chart setup posted each morning before the market opens

Chartworks

Web-based lessons and tutorials to Fibonacci and Beyond!

Enthios RealTime

A carefully selected suite of proprietary real-time indicators that form the Enthios System

Morning Call

A simple trade, once a day, for those with "other things to do."

FREE
Trial
Subscription

Visit www.**enthios**.com Today!

Free 2 Week Trial Offer for U.S. Residents From Investor's Business Daily:

INVESTOR'S BUSINESS DAILY will provide you with the facts, figures, and objective news analysis you need to succeed.

Investor's Business Daily is formatted for a quick and concise read to help you make informed and profitable decisions.

To take advantage of this free 2 week trial offer,
e-mail us at customerservice@traderslibrary.com
or visit our website at www.traderslibrary.com where
you find other free offers as well.

You can also reach us by calling 1-800-272-2855
or fax us at 410-964-0027.